Albert D. Kirwan

ALBERT D. KIRWAN

Frank Furlong Mathias

The University Press of Kentucky

ISBN: 978-0-8131-5323-0

Library of Congress Catalog Card Number: 74-18936

Copyright © 1975 by The University Press of Kentucky

A statewide cooperative scholarly publishing agency
serving Berea College, Centre College of Kentucky,
Eastern Kentucky University, Georgetown College,
Kentucky Historical Society, Kentucky State University,
Morehead State University, Murray State University,
Northern Kentucky State College, Transylvania University,
University of Kentucky, University 'of Louisville, and
Western Kentucky University.

Editorial and Sales Offices: Lexington, Kentucky 40506

To Florence, Nancy, Frank and Susan

Contents

Foreword ~ Clement Eaton   ix
Preface   xiii

I. A MAN FOR ALL SEASONS   1
  1. The Early Years   3
  2. The Coaching Years   19
  3. Dean Kirwan   32
  4. The Mature Leader   42
  Notes   67

II. WRITINGS & SPEECHES   73
  Introduction   75
  Education   79
  Civil War History   113
  Civil Rights   137
  Politics   157

  Index   187

Illustrations follow page 66

FOREWORD

Albert D. Kirwan, affectionately called "Ab" by his colleagues, was distinguished by a capacity for continuing growth in mind and personality until the very end of his life. In the academic world he was a "late bloomer," just as Abraham Lincoln and Jefferson Davis were. The early part of his career was spent in practicing law, coaching, and university administration, but these professions did not offer him the satisfactions for which he longed. He never made the pursuit of money a goal in life. He longed for culture and the satisfactions that university teaching, research, and writing brought him. His nature was a fine one, for it balanced in synthesis a rugged masculine personality with a high degree of sensitivity. He loved listening to opera on his radio, especially after his return from a year as Fulbright professor in Vienna, and much preferred it to seeing a football game on a television screen. He was sensitive also to the way people felt, which made him considerate of the persons with whom he came in contact, so that he was universally liked by colleagues and students.

A tall athletic man, with blue eyes framed by glasses, he had a commanding appearance and a quiet air of strength. His countenance was that of a fighter, a scholar, an Irish wit, and a kind human being. His powerful voice was a great asset in lecturing to the large classes that he taught toward the end of his life. His delightful sense of humor enlivened his lectures as well as his conversations with his colleagues. Democratic in manners, he had time for students, who felt that he was sympathetic to their problems. At the same time he showed, especially during the period when he was president of the University of Kentucky, that he had courage to do what he thought was right though it might cost him popularity among students.

His wife Betty was ideal for him. Vivacious, intelligent, and sympathetic, she accompanied him on his research trips, looked after his health, typed for him, and took notes on research materials. Indeed, Ab's family life was very attractive. I remember his telling me how he encouraged his boys to study by offering them as reward the use of the family car on certain nights if their grades were satisfactory. His system of incentives worked, for both of them became excellent students and later taught in good universities. Ab and Betty were gracious hosts in entertaining faculty and graduate students: the food was delicious; invigorating cocktails were served in silver julep cups; and best of all, one could enjoy conversation with some of the best minds of the University.

I used to admire Ab's firm discipline over himself. After his first heart attack he gave up smoking, but it was a struggle to do so. He regularly walked to and from his office. He worked hard, perhaps too hard, driven partly, I believe, by a desire to make up for lost time. He was so conscientious that when he went to historical meetings partly financed by University funds, he faithfully attended the sessions, while most of his colleagues skipped them to talk with historians from other universities or representatives of book companies.

Ab's contributions to southern history were important. His Ph.D. dissertation, written at Duke University, was a pathbreaker. Relatively few historians in America had concerned themselves with the history of poor people when he began his research for his dissertation, published under the title of *Revolt of the Rednecks: Mississippi Politics, 1876-1890.* In this book Ab showed great sympathy for and understanding of the submerged class of poor dirt farmers in the lower South and portrayed the demagogues as, despite their racist appeals, progressive in advocating social reforms. His prose was strong, lucid, and telling, and he displayed a rare critical talent in dealing with evidence. Professor Paul Gaston of the University of Virginia in a critical survey of writings on the New South praised it as "a model to be emulated by students of other states." After completing this book, Ab turned his attention to the history of the Confederacy and edited a delightful diary of a Kentucky soldier, entitled *Johnny Green of the Orphan Brigade,* followed by a collection of documents illustrating the social, economic, religious, and cultural developments in the Confederacy.

Next to *The Revolt of the Rednecks* his most significant work is his biography, *John J. Crittenden: The Struggle for the Union,* which received the Charles S. Sydnor Award of the Southern Historical Association. This superb work not only focuses on Crittenden as a Whig politician, but offers perhaps the best account of the efforts in Congress to compromise the issues between the South and the North just prior to the Civil War. His study of Crittenden led him to a decision to write a biography of Clay, and it is a great pity that he did not live to crown his historical career with a modern life of the great Kentucky statesman based on the collection of his papers now being published by the University Press of Kentucky. I remember talking with Ab about Henry Clay while he was doing research on the biography. He had a lower opinion of Clay than I had, and particularly criticized him as a politician for talking too much. I believe that, in addition to his academic training at Duke, his training as a lawyer would have given him a realistic insight into the career of "The Great Compromiser." His point of view as a historian was decidedly liberal, especially with respect to race relations, and this was reflected in his co-authorship with Thomas D. Clark of the text, *The South since Appomattox*.

In the untimely death of Albert D. Kirwan the southern historical profession lost one of its ablest members and the University of Kentucky and the Lexington community lost a splendid human being.

Clement Eaton

PREFACE

Great rivers form eddies and channels in the lives of men along their shores. Albert D. Kirwan was born not far from the Ohio River in 1904, and as a boy he frolicked and fished over its friendly surface. But it turned savagely upon him in 1913, when it flooded and destroyed his family's Louisville lumberyard. When he entered the University of Kentucky, he played football in a conference whose northern limits were marked by this great river. He coached with this same reference point in mind. As a Civil War historian he was constantly made aware of this stream as a divider between slavery and free soil, the setting for *Uncle Tom's Cabin,* and the scene of Morgan's cavalry crossings. Later, it separated the "Solid South" from the Republican North. Finally, as a teacher he could identify with students born along this beautiful, ever-moving northern border of Kentucky.

Blessed of great energy, heart, and mind, Albert Kirwan sooner or later wore most of the hats available in the field of higher education. He wore them exceedingly well, whether playing intercollegiate football, writing prizewinning history, or leading the University of Kentucky in one of its dark hours. Through it all he had the aid and comfort of a wife whose talents and charm were in no way inferior to his own. His story, then, is one of sports and scholarship, of family life and university administration. Finally, his is the story of a liberal Kentucky gentleman.

A large number of persons have generously helped me throughout the writing of this book. I wish first to express my heartfelt appreciation for the encouragement, help, and advice given me by Mrs. Albert D. Kirwan. I am most grateful, too, to Brit and Denny Kirwan for their help, and to Mr. William E. Kirwan and Mrs. Susan Kirwan McDevitt for interviews and letters that did much to explain the story of Ab's life. I thank the numerous persons who submitted to interviews, especially Dr. and Mrs. Carl Cone, Dr. James Hopkins, Dr. Lewis Cochran, Dr. Bennett Wall, Dr. Thomas D. Clark, Dean Wimberly Royster, Mr. Albert Tanner, Dr. Harry Denham, Coach Harry Lancaster, Mr. Bruce Denbo, Mrs. Rose Brumfield, Mrs. Harriet Van Meter, Mr. Earl Wallace, Dr. Donald Leigh, Dr. Stuart Forth, and Mr. Ray Bennett.

My thanks are due, too, to the staffs of several libraries: the University of Kentucky Library, where Mr. Charles Atcher aided me in the archives; the Louisville Public Library, with its fine collections of city material pertaining to the years of Kirwan's youth; and the University of Dayton Library, where Mr. Ray Nartker and his staff offered comfort as this book grew page by page in my carrel.

I am additionally indebted to the University of Dayton Research Council for several summer fellowships that made possible a much earlier completion of this volume than was at first anticipated. My colleague, Dr. Leroy Eid, lightened my departmental duties whenever possible and encouraged me throughout the enterprise.

Finally, my appreciation in fullest measure goes to my wife Florence. Her patience, help, and understanding have made smooth the path for an early finish to a most enjoyable task.

I.

A Man for All Seasons

1. THE EARLY YEARS

There was one thing about young Albert Dennis Kirwan that his brother Will, two years his elder, did not like—and that was his name. Try as he might, "Albert" always came out "Abbert." Catherine and Patrick, the two younger children, shortened this to "Ab." This simple yet distinctive name stuck with Kirwan throughout his life, forever baffling acquaintances who tried to derive "Ab" from either "A. D." or "Albert."

The Kirwan name probably first appeared in Louisville around 1850, when Patrick Nolan Kirwan, Albert's grandfather, came down the Ohio River with his brother Edward looking for a place to settle. In choosing Louisville, they ended a hectic journey from Galway, Ireland. Seven Kirwan brothers had fled the Irish potato famine of the late 1840s and landed in North Carolina, but except for Patrick and Edward, each went his separate way.

Patrick and Edward arrived in Louisville during an era of nativist hostility and occasional rioting against immigrants. Patrick not only weathered the troubled 1850s, but also found a wife. In 1857 he married Mary Elizabeth Ross, whose family had come to Kentucky from Maryland after the Revolution. Between 1858 and his untimely death in 1865, Mary bore Patrick six children; the second, Martin John, born in 1859, was to be the father of Albert Dennis Kirwan.[1]

Martin's widowed mother, hard pressed to support her six young children, insisted that they contribute to the family's upkeep as soon as they were employable. Martin, the oldest son, led the way by securing various part-time jobs as a youngster. In 1877 he won his first permanent job as a clerk in a small lumberyard owned by his cousin Edward and a friend. Although this fragile concern folded in 1881, forcing Martin to clerk for the Louisville and Nashville Railroad until 1885, dealing in lumber was to be his life's work.

Despite his mother's opposition, Martin married Minnie Jones in 1888. Mary Elizabeth Kirwan was a very possessive and strong-willed woman, and she hated to surrender any of her boys to matrimony. Six years later she would oppose Martin's second marriage just as bluntly as she had his first. Martin's brother Joseph went so far as to postpone his own marriage until after Mrs. Kirwan's death in 1915. Martin, however, had much of his mother's will, and set his own course in spite of her protests. Over the next four years Minnie bore three boys: Edward Emmett in 1889, Harry in 1891, and Joseph

Ross in 1892. The responsibilities of a growing family induced Martin to start his own lumberyard in 1892; the next year he took Joseph on as a partner, and the enterprise became Kirwan Brothers Lumber Company. Although Martin's total investment washed away in the 1913 flood, his brother Joseph and others managed to rebuild and continue the company until 1962.

Following Minnie's death during childbirth, Martin courted Margaret Sullivan, a charming woman six years his junior. They were married in 1896, and her three stepsons welcomed her into their Franklin Street home. "Margaret became a devoted mother to the three boys and they in turn loved her as deeply as they could have their own mother." In 1897 Margaret gave the boys a half-sister, Mary; in 1898 another, Margaret; and finally a half-brother, named for Martin, in 1899. Martin and Margaret now purchased a large frame house at 1842 Mellwood Avenue, and the family moved there in 1900. Accessible to both the Kirwan lumberyard and the home of Martin's brother Joe at 1534 Fulton Street, it was located just south of River Road in "The Point," a two-square-mile area along what was then Louisville's eastern edge, centering on Beargrass Creek's confluence with the Ohio River.[2] The Fischer Packing Company building now stands on the spot once occupied by Martin's house.

By now, Martin had moved into the upper middle class, for the lumberyard at Fulton and Adams streets was a very profitable business. He and Margaret had a stable of excellent horses, a carriage, several buggies, and enjoyed a well-equipped household. As far as the children were concerned, having a lumberman for a father was blessing enough. They were thrilled by the whirring, screaming sound of giant saws biting into hardwood, and they loved the hot pungent odor of freshly sawed pine. There were great logs in the river to skip across, huge mounds of sawdust for tumbling on, friendly workers to talk with and to tease them. They were proud of their father and Uncle Joe, saw their name in advertisements: Kirwan Brothers—manufacturing blinds, sashes, doors, frames, and moldings; dealing in lumber "rough or dressed."

Martin's family continued to grow. The first twentieth-century child was Susan, who arrived in 1901. Two years later Margaret gave birth to her fifth child, and Martin's eighth, William English. A ninth was expected in December 1904. Everyone waited eagerly for the new arrival—perhaps the baby would arrive on Christmas Day! Thursday, December 22, was unseasonably warm, with a temperature of 58 degrees under an overcast sky; so Dr. James Pell had no difficulty reaching the Kirwan home in time to help Margaret deliver a boy, promptly named Albert Dennis.

The city Albert would know so well as a boy and young man exuded optimism and progress in 1904. The Masonic Temple and the Jewish Hospital were completed that year, and both a new jail was under construction and buildings for the fire-ravaged Bourbon Stockyards. Broadway and Chestnut streets were opened all the way to Shawnee Park, and many new brick streets were being built elsewhere. The Louisville Railway Company, serving a city of 228,500 people, was proud to replace its "squat, cold cars" with "imposing, roomy, heated cars." A nickel fare with transfer would take one "to almost any point on the entire system." Business was good, and labor strife, though troublesome in some cities, was "only slightly felt in Louisville." In short, things looked good for a person born in 1904; the last rosy glow of the old order had a decade to go before World War I changed the world forever.

Martin and Margaret were good parents. Relaxed and easygoing, Margaret created a bond of love and confidence with her children that endured until her death. Backing her was a husband who would "use an old razor strop" to curb childish misbehavior, but who was "very kindly and gentle as a rule." Ab revealed years later that Martin was much more than a disciplinarian:

> At nighttime, my father would sit around the fire with all of the children and my mother gathered there, and he would read to us. Although this started when I was a young child and I never understood the plot or the progress of the story, nevertheless I was entranced, and all of us were entranced with the reading of my father. . . . He read to us most of Charles Dickens, . . . Thackeray, Robert Louis Stevenson, Fenimore Cooper, some of Shakespeare, and Mark Twain's *Huckleberry Finn* and *Tom Sawyer*. . . . I think it taught all of us to have a great love for literature.[3]

Ab was seven in 1912, when the family moved to an antebellum three-story brick house at 326 East Jacob Street. This fifteen-room home was near the center of Louisville in a "better neighborhood" than The Point. Uncle Joe and Grandma Kirwan remained at 1534 Fulton, however, and therein lay a problem for Ab and Will. Uncle

Joe always kept cows on his land, and Martin's family had long been drinking that milk. Since the cows could not come to Jacob Street, Ab and Will had to go to the cows. Each took his daily turn carrying and sloshing a heavy pail of milk two miles to the family table. One can imagine the condition of the milk when it arrived! Will still remembers it as "one of the meanest jobs we had in those days."

Ab's competitive spirit revealed itself early in frequent fights with Martin, Jr.—this in a relatively peaceful household. The older Martin would often thrash both Ab and Will at the same time! Will eventually had "sense enough to know Martin could whip me, but Ab didn't." For Ab this was not a matter of "sense"—he had plenty of that—but a matter of attitude and self-testing. He'd fight Martin, get whipped, and then tell Will: "I just don't understand how in the world Martin can take such punishment!" This frame of mind later made him a formidable athlete, and with the balance that came with maturity, it provided the determination to achieve undertakings others might have hesitated even to attempt.

Martin Kirwan would not allow his children to start school until they were nine years old. They were then expected to make up for lost time and finish elementary school at fourteen. An exception was made for Ab, who started at seven so that he and nine-year-old Will could be together. All of the children except young Pat went to Blessed Sacrament, a two-room parochial school in The Point. Two nuns taught about fifty students, and one of these was Sister Mary Henry. She was the sister of Martin's first wife, thus a true aunt only to Ab's half-brothers, but all of the children considered her to be their Aunt Pet.

Aunt Pet's misguided partiality toward nieces and nephews caused much trouble. Finding Ab to be a good reader, she started him in the second grade. This still left him below his reading level, however, and so the next year she moved him through the third, fourth, and fifth grades. Although he remained in the sixth grade a full year, he skipped the seventh and eighth grades and entered St. Xavier High School when he was ten years old! Will, who had accompanied him through this accelerated schooling, was all of twelve.

Ab and Will spent nearly seven years in high school, first at St. Xavier and then at Male after the family finances failed to recover from the flood damage of 1913. Martin now worked as an estimator for Frey Lumber Company, a former competitor. At night he tried to instruct Ab and Will in the ways of high school. These two, clad in knee pants, heavy socks, and high black shoes, wandered the high school halls, sitting down in any classroom having vacant seats. Whenever the bell rang, they got up and repeated the process. It took them almost three years to earn enough credits to become sophomores. Ab later recalled:

> I can remember so well my father trying to help us solve our algebra problems.... On one occasion my poor father worked for perhaps a half-hour solving a problem, and I looked at it and said, "No, that's the wrong answer." So my father went back to work and checked everything and came up with the same answer, equal to ten in the problem he worked. He finally asked me how I knew the problem was wrong, and I said, "Because the teacher worked a problem today and the answer came out $x=6$"! This is merely an indication of how little I understood.

Tragedy first entered Ab's life in 1917. Grandma Sullivan, who had been living with Martin's family, died in their Jacob Street home that summer. But death was to strike an even sharper double blow to the young boy and his family before the year was out. Ab's oldest and youngest sisters, Mary and Catherine, had been ill for several months. It was known that vivacious Mary had tuberculosis, but Catherine's problem defied diagnosis. Medical treatment seemed to have no effect. Ab later believed the ten-year-old child "had congenital heart disease." She died in December 1917, and the next month the blow was compounded immeasurably by the death of the beloved oldest sister. The family had thus sustained three deaths in a period of six months.

These deaths, coming after a year of strenuous nursing and care, utterly exhausted Ab's mother. Ab and Will decided to help her as best they could. Both delivered the *Courier-Journal* each morning and returned home before the others were even out of bed. And soon they were cooking breakfast to save their mother the task. Years later, Ab's sons were destined to hear many times of his prowess in making biscuits: "In that day, of course, one didn't have prepared biscuits. One had to get the flour from the barrel, sift it, mix in lard and knead it, mix in a little baking powder, salt, and pour in milk gradually while kneading the dough. I must say that I made very good biscuits. Betty has never really believed that, but I did!"

Margaret now emerged as the acknowledged leader of Martin's second family. Although reared as Catholics, all except one followed the strong-willed big sister in her permanent drift away from Catholicism. Her older half-brothers, of course, were free of her influence, and they remained Catholics throughout their lives. Family harmony never suffered, for they all respected one another's views and did not question one another as to the rights or wrongs of individual actions.

Ab's great natural athletic ability rescued him from the pathetic shyness he had developed as an underage high school student. He had begun playing football in the spacious sideyard of his Jacob Street home, and soon became so much better than his playmates that he had to pay them to play against him. Although he received a weekly allowance of only twenty-five cents, he paid it out gladly every Saturday to hire players at a nickel each.

In September 1920, a broad, rangy-framed 135-pounder, Ab tried out for the Male football team. Coach Howard Wiles recognized the boy's desire and ability, and announced that Ab would play end position in the starting line-up. His dreams had come true! He played every minute of the first five contests. In the 1920s, a game lasted sixty minutes, and once taken out, a player could not return during that half; so coaches dared not remove any of their regulars until the game was safely won. In short, high school football at that time was a more rugged game than it is today.

An ankle injury prevented Ab from making more than a token appearance in the annual Thanksgiving Day game with duPont Manual High School, Male's great and bitter crosstown rival. His Purples inflicted a 21-13 upset on what was probably a superior but improperly coached Crimson team.[4] "But then the dream of dreams came true at the football banquet the following week," Ab recalled later. The seniors returned from a fifteen-minute post-banquet huddle to announce that they had elected Ab Kirwan to captain the Purples for 1921! "The rest of the year I was on cloud nine."

Male's 1921 team went undefeated through its first nine games. Kirwan had been shifted from end to fullback, and played the entire season from that position. But after the ninth game, Dr. Pell put Ab to bed with a badly infected knee, telling him that once again he would be unable to play in the great Thanksgiving Day game with Manual. This was terrible news, but on Wednesday morning the young fullback was ready to believe in miracles—the swelling had left his knee. He ran the few blocks from his home to Male to attend the huge pregame pep rally. The team was on a platform, and the best of the alumni orators were exhorting both players and students. "The principal, Mr. J. B. Carpenter, had already announced that I would not be able to play the next day, when I walked in. The minute I did, he saw me and called me to the platform, and as I took my place there, the student body gave me such an ovation as I have never had since and never expect to have. It was one of the truly memorable moments in my life."

Two undefeated teams took to a muddy field at Eclipse Park for the 1921 game, with Manual the favorite. Crimson supporters, rankled by last year's upset, had hired a new coach, Neal Arntson. Manual gained 273 yards to Male's 62, but a gritty Purple defense always stopped them short of the goal line. Purple-clad Ab was soon caked with mud, and the newspapers later reported almost monotonously: "In two tries at center, Kirwan made a total of four yards.... Kirwan slid through tackle for three yards.... Kirwan could not gain at center.... Kirwan was hurt on the play, but resumed his position.... Kirwan fumbled the ball and the Crimson recovered.... Kirwan's pass grounded ... ," and so it went, for "the Male offense had little power."[5] When the gun sounded the end of the fray, the two teams were still undefeated—they had fought to a scoreless tie. Even this moral victory for Male High School was a keen disappointment to the players.

About the time Ab finished high school in 1922, his parents moved the five children remaining at home to a smaller house at 159 North Hite Avenue. Whereupon Harry and Joseph, who were now working, also moved to this pleasant street in Crescent Hill.[6] The family genuinely enjoyed one another's company, and regularly gathered at Martin's house to visit and play table games. Will, a storeclerk at this time, recalls the "regular weekend bridge party. We'd just go on from Saturday afternoon until late Sunday night without a break." During this time, Ab developed into a skilled competitor. Throughout his life, bridge was his best and favorite game, but he was always ready to take anyone on in checkers, chess, cribbage, Monopoly, or any table game they might name or even invent.

In the autumn of 1922 Ab started classes at the University of Kentucky. His football record had brought him "offers from many colleges," but he had already made up his mind that he would not attend any school very far from his aging parents.

> The idea of Centre College at first intrigued me because of the great football program they had there. This was the day of Bo McMillan, Red Roberts, Red Weaver, and a host of other stars, and Centre had made a national reputation. ... I had been visited by Bo McMillan in the summer of 1922, and he suggested that I might do well by going to Centre. ... My sister Margaret, however, was very much opposed to my going to Centre. She was, although a young woman, the registrar at the University of Louisville, ... and she was definitely of the opinion that football was stressed too much at Centre. On the other hand, she was quite impressed with the academic quality at the University of Kentucky, particularly the engineering program there, and I had, for some reason or other, had some interest at the time in studying engineering. So she urged me to go to the University of Kentucky, and finally I made up my mind I would do so.

"For some reason or other" Ab had convinced himself that engineering was an acceptable substitute for playing with the famous Centre Colonels! His emotional yearnings in 1922 were those of a fullback, yet his strong sense of loyalty guided him into accepting Margaret's seemingly logical advice. Ab's wife Betty offers a more realistic appraisal of what happened: "His sister wanted him to go into engineering because 'that is how you make money.' Margaret ... had different values than Ab—making money wasn't a consideration *ever* in his life. He stuck to engineering for three and one-half years, but because he loved English, he switched colleges and was able to graduate with an A.B. degree with a major in English."

Ab caught a ride to Lexington with a returning student. When they neared the University campus, the driver pulled in at the Sigma Nu fraternity house. Ab was invited in, met the brothers, and was offered a room for a few days. He had not thought much about fraternities, but soon he was favorably impressed. There was no social program arranged by the University, nor was sufficient housing available, so the fraternities and sororities filled a definite need at the school. Although he was invited to pledge Sigma Nu, Ab at first refused for fear it would be too expensive. There were no athletic scholarships, and he was paying his own way. However, when the fraternity then offered him the job of dining room manager—ordering food and planning meals in return for room and board—Ab accepted, convinced that fraternity life would cost him no more than living elsewhere. "So I pledged the Sigma Nu fraternity and must say that it added a great deal to the contentment, the pleasure, and the happiness of my life while I was at the University."

The University of Kentucky of 1922 was almost completely an undergraduate institution, with very few areas in which one might work toward a master's degree. The campus had no more than twenty buildings, and the only women's dormitory was located on Limestone Street. The place was small enough to meet the same people often in class or on campus, so a friendly atmosphere prevailed between the 1,800 students and some 200 faculty members.

Ab, of course, went to college during the "Roaring Twenties." The nondrinking and unsuspecting young athlete soon discovered that "there was a great deal of drinking among university students; this was, of course, during the Prohibition years." The first weekend in his fraternity house found him doctoring hangovers and other sicknesses that some of the boys had contracted from drinking illicit liquor. Ab felt "they had simply been caught in a predicament they would not repeat," but he soon found that these same fellows came in drunk every weekend.

Notwithstanding its few weekend drunks, the University fell far short of the "jazz age" college scenes depicted by F. Scott Fitzgerald. Very few of Ab's contemporaries had an automobile, and Ab himself walked wherever he went. Usually his footprints could be followed to one or the other of the two celebrated college hangouts: Polis's Restaurant, a small short-order place at the corner of Euclid and Limestone, or if he craved more company, the Lexington Drug, situated in a now demolished wing of the Phoenix Hotel on Main Street. "It was such a common gathering place that one could leave a message for almost anyone in the University student body to be delivered, and be pretty certain that the message would reach the person it was intended for."

Ab was soon taking part in the school's social life. The fraternities required their freshmen to attend the open houses held by each sorority every Sunday afternoon. However, all University men were invited, whether they were in a fraternity or not. A rather shy Ab attended "under compulsion" at first, but this phase soon passed, and he "became acquainted with some very fine young women who have been friends of mine throughout my lifetime." After football season, he sought out the Saturday afternoon dances sponsored by different University clubs and organizations. These were held variously in the Patterson Hall dining room, in the Armory, or on the basketball floor of Alumni Gymnasium, which was finished in 1924. "This," Ab later recalled, "was before Coach [Adolph] Rupp's time. You would never think of permitting dances to be held on his basketball floor!"

Ab was greatly impressed by certain teachers, and his descriptions of them reveal something of the University's academic life during this era:

> There were certain celebrated figures on the faculty at that time, so-called great men, that students were urged to have a course under, or else one thought that his college career would not be fully developed. One of these men was Dr. [William H.] Funkhouser, . . . a biologist and one of the best lecturers in the University. . . . He used to come to class with snakes that he wished to demonstrate certain things about, and he would have these snakes wrapped around his body inside his shirt and when the appropriate time came he would simply unbutton his shirt and pull out a snake. . . . Another one of these men whose fame was great among the students was Professor William S. Webb, whom we all called "Bullneck." He was a wonderful lecturer [in Physics], and although a very fine and a very gentle person, his course in sophomore physics . . . was a terror to many of the students. . . . There was, of course, [E. F.] "Red" Farquhar, the magnificent lecturer in English literature.
>
> I had the opportunity to take in all of these men. I can still hear "Red" Farquhar, with that flaming red hair that matched the color of his florid face, tossing his head aside as he would cite verses from Tennyson or indeed verses from the Bible. He had a course in the history of the Bible that was a very popular one. Then there was [Ralph N.] "Maggie" Maxson, the terror of the students in chemistry. On one occasion, a student who had been away for some years came back . . . and said something no student ought ever to say to a former professor: "You don't remember me do you?" Maxson turned a cold eye

on him, looked over the top of his spectacles and said, "Young man, you are the type of student that I spend many years trying to forget."

The students of this era stood in great awe of President Frank LeRond McVey. He even looked the part of a president, tall and slender, with a long, dignified, intellectual face. He was a gentle person, yet his presence communicated a feeling of austerity and dignity. Kirwan's following account reveals much about President McVey, about Ab himself, and, incidentally, about the kind of relationship a student leader maintained with a college president in the 1920s:

> During the course of my career at the university, I found myself, for one reason or another, being ushered into his presence with some kind of a petition which I had had little to do with formulating, and indeed knew little about.... Students used to petition in those days, much as they make demands now.
> Dr. McVey would take me into his inner office. He would sit me down. He would look calmly over the petition that I had presented, and he would look up and talk to me in a very calm, dignified voice for five or ten minutes. At the end of that time, I would find myself out in the hall, not remembering much of what he had said, but being sure that the answer to the petition was no.

President McVey's wife, Frances Jewell, was greatly loved by the students. She was dean of women, and had married McVey after the death of his first wife. In Ab's opinion, "she was greater, perhaps, as a president's wife even than he was as a president." She entertained brilliantly and frequently, setting every Wednesday afternoon aside to serve tea at an open house for students.

It was a hot afternoon in late summer when Kentucky's 1922 football squad met for its first practice. The athletics director, S. A. "Daddy" Boles, was surprised to see Ab Kirwan walk into his office and apply for a uniform. He knew who he was, but since Kentucky did nothing in the way of recruiting or supporting athletics, Boles assumed Centre or some other college had signed Male's star fullback.⁷ Ab got his uniform in what was probably record-breaking speed on Boles's part.

When Ab first slipped his 185 pounds into Kentucky's blue uniform, he was unknowingly taking his first step toward being the school's president. But at the moment, self-doubts about his ability to make a college team plagued him. Kentucky was one of twenty schools forming the Southern Intercollegiate Conference, and a ruling the previous year forbade the use of freshmen against varsity teams in 1922. Fifty-five men tried out for Kentucky's first freshman team, coached by E. B. "Dick" Webb. Ab starred, and although a local sportswriter misspelled his name, he left no doubt regarding Kirwan's performance: "A. Kirvan, fullback off Louisville Male High, is the best looking football player, barring none, that has been on Stoll Field for a generation.... The varsity line just couldn't stop him."⁸

Kentucky's 1922 freshmen lost only one game, a better record than the varsity's six wins and three losses. Photographs of Captain Kirwan reveal him typically attired in high hip pads, striped socks, dusty ankle-top shoes, and vertical stripes running high up the chest of his jersey. He had a slight bow in his legs, was a bit nearsighted, and wore a distinctive peaked helmet that many fans would soon recognize.

Certain games endured in Ab's memory as "highlights of my career." In his speeches, he usually set the stage for younger audiences this way: "Many of [these games] have to do with Centre College and a few of them with the University of Tennessee.... Centre was truly our great rival in that day, and Centre was much the best team we played against year after year. I know it's a little difficult for people to realize that now who didn't live at that time.... But there was a ten-year period from 1916 to 1925 when Kentucky not only had never beaten Centre, but indeed they had not scored a touchdown against Centre."

Centre played at home to win the first of two freshman games with Kentucky in 1922. Three weeks after this 14-6 victory, the Lieutenants visited the Kittens on Stoll Field, which at that time occupied the parking area now behind the Student Center. The Sigma Nu house, where Ab lived, occupied a small bluff above the corner of Euclid and Harrison avenues, offering a perfect view over the fence of the playing field to its front. Indeed, Ab often brought Albert Tanner, a black child, to his window to watch the games.

Tanner later became butler at Maxwell Place, and years after, was butler to Ab himself. In any event, Captain Kirwan thrilled the fans and his small friend in the window by scoring twice on short runs to lead the Kittens to a 19-0 victory over the Centre freshmen.[9]

Ab won a position on the 1923 varsity team, coached by Jack Winn, a former Princeton star. Although Ab played throughout this mediocre 4-3-2 season, once again, the games that best endured in his memory were those against Centre and Tennessee.

Kentucky helped Centre dedicate its new stadium that year—Cheek Field. Ab played left halfback as the Wildcats lost 10-0 "before a crowd of 10,000 of the wettest fans who ever witnessed a football game."[10] Centre's gold-and-white warriors were soon mud-caked, but they kept Kentucky on the defensive throughout the game. Ab so seldom got past the line of scrimmage that he finished the game with an average yardage of minus two. Years later, he finally heard the story behind his dismal showing: "I ran into Minos Gordy, ... who played offensive fullback and defensive end for them. I asked [him] ... what happened to me that day; it worried me. . . . 'Well,' he said 'after the first few plays when the color of our uniforms was completely obliterated by the mud, ... our two guards would line up with your team and . . . simply turn around and tackle you!' . . . I'm inclined to believe that he might have been telling the truth."

What might well have been a turning point in Ab's life came as a result of the 1923 Tennessee game. The Volunteers' prowess was such that they had beaten little Georgetown College by only one touchdown the previous Saturday. Kentucky was favored, yet nothing went right for Captain Kirwan and his men. Quarterback Turner Gregg called on Ab three times in one series of plays to carry the ball over from the two-yard line. Ab failed. Later he fumbled into a Volunteer's arms for a score. Orangemen blocked a Wildcat goal-line punt and fell on it in the end zone for another score. Finally, a Kentucky pass was intercepted and run back for a Vol touchdown. Tennessee won 18-0.[11]

Ab accepted his bad luck as part of the game, but the next day signs sprouted around the campus reading, "TENNESSEE 18, SIGMA NU 0," an allusion to the fact that Quarterback Gregg and Ab were fraternity brothers. This was too much for young Ab to bear. He wrote to his old Male teammate, Edliff "Butch" Slaughter, who was well on his way to becoming an all-American at Michigan:

"I asked him about the possibility and prospect of my . . . coming to the University of Michigan." Slaughter responded very favorably, "but my old friend and [backfield] coach Doc Rodes talked me out of it. . . . I decided I would remain at Kentucky, and it was one of the wisest decisions that I have ever made."

Ab believed the Centre squad of 1924 "was maybe the best team that Centre ever had. It's true Bo McMillan and Red Roberts were gone, but they had very fine backs in Herb Covington and in my old friend Minos Gordy." Centre went on to win the Southern championship that year, beating such teams as Alabama and Georgia. Kentucky's new coach, Fred Murphy, couldn't stop them either. As one sportswriter put it: "Covington and Gordy did more things to the Kentucky line than a laundry can do to a silk shirt!" Although the final score was 7-0, Centre "was better by more than by a mere touchdown."[12]

Captain Kirwan's senior season in 1925 was his most satisfying. This year Kentucky had a Halloween date with Centre, a team they had not scored on since 1916. The game was hardly underway on muddy Cheek Field when the Wildcat quarterback made a long run to the Colonels' two-yard line. He then handed off to Kirwan, his right halfback, and Ab quite literally disappeared under a huge pileup on the goal line. The officials were going to have to unravel the mass of gold and blue uniforms before 12,000 frantic fans would know if the Centre jinx had been ended. Down on the bottom, with his left arm pinned and his right arm around the ball, Ab knew the ball was clearly over the goal line. But suddenly the hand of a Centre lineman slithered across Ab's face and started oozing the muddy ball out of his right arm. Ab was desperate; "I reached over and bit him on the arm!" The bellowing lineman cleared several players away as he leaped to his feet, giving the official ample room to see that Ab had possession and to rule a touchdown. Meanwhile, the lineman showed the referee Ab's toothmarks on his arm. Ab admitted it, explaining the circumstances. The referee then said, "Let's play ball," whereupon the Wildcat team put a 16-0 "bite" on Centre for the first time in a decade.[13]

Ab hung up his blue uniform for the last time after the 1925 Tennessee game. This savagely contested game was decided in the fourth quarter. By then, the Wildcats had scored three touchdowns, two of them on passes from Kirwan, and the score was 20-13. As the fourth quarter opened, Kentucky kicked a field goal after three futile downs on the Volunteer's seven-yard line. But Tennessee was offside on the play, and the referee asked Captain Kirwan if he wanted the penalty or the three points. Ab was in a quandry: "If I took the penalty, the ball would be placed on Tennessee's two-yard line, and we would have four downs in which to make the two yards. From what had been happening that afternoon, I had no real confidence that we would make that two yards." Finally, as the referee pressured him, he took the field goal, for "I made up my mind that if we couldn't hold a ten-point lead for fifteen minutes, we didn't deserve to win."

The next fifteen minutes were the longest of Ab's young life. Following Kentucky's kickoff, the Vols quickly added seven more points, and the score was 23-20. They then forced the Wildcats to punt, and with two minutes to go they had moved to a first down on Kentucky's two-yard line. Ab would be the goat of the game if they scored for his having taken the three points instead of trying for a touchdown. During a time-out Ab gave his team what may have been the best lecture of his life. His men then lined up against the powerful Tennessee offense and stopped them cold for four downs straight! In a few seconds "the game was over and we had won 23 to 20 in one of the truly memorable Tennessee-Kentucky games."[14] Indeed, the Wildcats were to beat the Volunteers only once more during the two decades following this victory. The old Centre jinx was replaced by the Tennessee jinx, a fact Ab later had to live with when he became the Wildcat coach.

Although football made Ab a well-known campus figure, it demanded much time and energy each autumn. He won letters in track too, thus losing even more time to athletics. He participated in Romany plays, was active in Lamp and Cross, and in 1925 helped found the University chapter of Omicron Delta Kappa, a fraternal society honoring student leadership. Besides this, he had his daily task in the Sigma Nu dining room, and for a while he worked as an assistant in the dean of men's office. All these demands upon Kirwan's time hurt his academic record. He graduated with a cumulative grade average of C+, a mark that did not reflect his keen intellectual ability. Others of course have overcome equal demands on their time to make outstanding academic records, but Ab had little incentive to do so; as his widow points out: "Ab should never have been in engineering—he couldn't even put up a curtain rod!"

It is not surprising, then, that the end of Ab's college football career brought a crisis—did he really want to devote his life to engineering? He decided that he did not, and considered entering the Kentucky law school, changing his academic major to English with this in mind. Although he was permitted to graduate with his class in June 1926, he had to attend summer school to complete 15 required credits in English. As a result, he did not receive his A.B. degree until December 14, 1926. Meanwhile, he had decided against going to law school; instead, he remained as an assistant in Dean C. R. Melcher's office and helped his former coach with the football team.

2. THE COACHING YEARS

Coach Murphy hired Ab as his backfield coach in 1926. Kentucky had graduated many veterans in addition to Kirwan, and the 1926 season was to end with two wins, six losses, and one tie. Though explainable enough, this poor record brought Kirwan's first experience with disgruntled alumni. The weekend before the annual Thanksgiving Day game with Tennessee, some of the alumni members of the athletics board persuaded the president to call an athletics board meeting and ordered Murphy to turn over his job to an interim coach.

However, the alumni coup turned sour when the team found out what had happened: they vehemently refused to play Tennessee unless Murphy was reinstated. Such refusal would not only have blemished the good name of the University, but also required payment of a considerable sum of money to the Knoxville institution. A hasty meeting of the athletics board was called and signals were reversed. Murphy was implored to resume charge of the team. "He did," Ab explained, "as the gentleman that he was." But he made it clear to all that after the Knoxville trip he was through, and "if offered a new contract he would not accept."[15]

The outraged Wildcats played a grand game against a superior Tennessee eleven, but went down to a 6-0 loss. Ab, Murphy, and the team then made their way back to Lexington: "I packed my gear and left the city very discouraged at this very unhappy event that had marred my very last experience, I thought, at the University of Kentucky. Although I loved the institution and the community dearly, I felt that this had left a scar that . . . even time would not heal."

College life ended abruptly for Ab. While the football season was grinding to its ignoble end, Kirwan secured a job with the Midcontinental Petroleum Corporation. It would enable him to repay the $700 or so that he had borrowed from the University to finish school. On the first day of December 1926, the 21-year-old ex-football star, ex-backfield coach, ex-engineering student, and all-around ex-"bigman-on-campus" sighed as he clasped a "useless" English degree and went to work promoting Diamond brand oil and gasoline throughout southern Illinois. This was during the Prohibition era and the region, often called "Little Egypt," was embroiled in a war between two rival gangs of rumrunners. Ab's experiences were so varied and colorful that by the spring of 1927 he decided to quit and enter the University of Kentucky law school. "With this end in view, I had written to my dear old friend, the dean of men, Columbus Rudolph Melcher, and he had promised me a position in his office as assistant dean of men. This would pay my expenses to law school." Family responsibilities prevented Ab from accepting this offer, but twenty years later, when he was tendered the position of dean of men, he did not hesitate to take it.

Ab returned to Louisville to find his father bedfast and his health deteriorating to the extent that death claimed him in 1929. He had come home to help, and so immediately set to looking for a job, but he had hardly begun when J. B. Carpenter, his old high school principal, sent for him. Ab quickly accepted Carpenter's offer to teach English at Male and serve as assistant football coach. Although coaching was to claim Ab for fifteen more years, now he was delighted to discover his great ability as a classroom teacher. His obvious love of teaching, his honesty, and the ease with which he presented his subject won students to his side as quickly here as they did later at Manual and at the University of Kentucky. As if coaching and teaching were not enough, he then enrolled for night classes at the Jefferson School of Law. Ab taught five classes of English daily, helped coach football until 5:30 p.m., rushed home to eat, and then sat in law classes from seven until nine o'clock. After that he often visited his head coach, Tom Johnson, and these two bachelors would talk football late into the night.

Johnson and Kirwan worked well together, producing winning teams at Male from 1927 through 1931. Notably, Manual never scored on the Purples during this period, although they earned a scoreless tie in 1930. Ab was not head coach, but he was being watched as a young man with an extremely keen football sense.[16]

Few things could have distracted Ab from his steady round of teaching, coaching, law classes, and bridge playing—but romance was one of them. He had long known the Heil family who lived out in Crescent Hill, for John Heil had been a classmate at Male and was now enrolled with him in law school. Moreover, young Alan Heil had tagged around after Ab during the several summers Ab worked as a lifeguard at Crescent Hill Pool. Alan was now proudly enrolled in his hero's English class at Male. When John Heil started bringing Ab and Henry Brooks—all three former Male classmates—home after classes to play three-handed bridge, it was not long before Ab began to notice another member of the household, his friend's charming and vivacious sister Elizabeth.

Betty Heil was two years younger than Ab. She had entered DePauw University in 1923, where she pledged Kappa Kappa Gamma sorority, and finished her degree in Romance languages in 1927 at the University of Louisville. Now she was teaching at Shawnee High School while her fiancé, a former teammate of Ab's at Kentucky, was spending two years at Oxford University on a Rhodes scholarship.

The card games continued at the Heil home, but soon John Heil and Henry Brooks were left playing a two-handed game, for Ab had deserted bridge for Betty. Ab wanted to get married right away, but Betty had promised to await her fiancé's return. Shortly thereafter, on August 14, 1931, Ab and Betty were married in Louisville's First Presbyterian Church.[17]

Ab found much to like in his father-in-law, John H. Heil. A Louisville insurance man, Heil had earlier coached high school football in Muskegon, Michigan, and Moline, Illinois. His great day as a coach had come in 1902, when Moline beat Galva High School 172 to 0. Heil's halfback, Harvey Kelting, scored the point after touchdown thirteen times straight, missed two, and then made fourteen more in a row. This feat made Robert Ripley's newspaper feature, "Believe-It-or-Not," and probably still stands in the football record book.[18] In any event, whenever Ab took Betty to visit her old home at 1590 Cherokee Road, he and Dad Heil never had the least trouble communicating with each other.

When Ab brought his bride back from their North Carolina honeymoon and carried her into their house on Birchwood Avenue in Crescent Hill, he was nearly 27 years old and still undecided as to his life's work. Although Ab had won his law degree and was admitted to the bar, he taught and coached at Male one more year; meanwhile, he tried to get a start as a lawyer. Ab, Henry Brooks, and William "Babe" Lawson had opened a law office at 512 Inter-Southern Life Building. Years later they would laugh about the fact that Ab had finished first in the class while Brooks had graduated somewhere near the bottom; yet Ab quit the legal field and Brooks went on to become a federal judge. But there was little laughter now, in 1931, for the Great Depression was nearing its depth. The trio waited hungrily for a tug on their web.

One day, while Ab was minding the desk, an old riverman

shuffled into the lawyers' lair. He had come through the first door he saw with an attorney's sign on it. He was from aboard the steamboat *Martha,* he said, and his wages had not been paid. Moreover, there were thirty more like him back on the boat. He wanted to file a mechanic's lien against the owners. Ab took the case, although "I didn't know land law, much less maritime law." But he got his books out and went to work. Since national waterways were involved, the case was tried in a federal court. "I didn't know what I was doing," Ab always confessed when relating the tale, "but old Judge [Charles I.] Dawson practiced it for me." Ab won the case, but "I was so excited that when Judge Dawson said 'sign here,' I didn't even know where to sign." Kirwan received a $2,000 fee, a huge sum in those days.[19]

Ab's choice of a legal career looked much better after this case, yet he was unable to shake a growing conviction that his future lay elsewhere, that he could not accept law as his life's work. He therefore had no hesitation about closing his legal desk forever on that day in 1932 when he was offered Neal Arntson's position as head coach of the Manual Crimson football team.

Kirwan had no sooner abandoned law and settled into the company of his fellow athletes than he became uneasy again. Throughout his life he always experienced misgivings whenever he was unable to use one or another of his markedly superior abilities in athletics, scholarship, and administration. His drive to excel dictated that he attempt to juggle many activities, keeping all of his talents simultaneously in motion. Coaching may have satisfied his athletic yearnings, but it offered scant outlet for his other great skills. Sensing this, Kirwan began to take undergraduate courses in history and education at the University of Louisville while he was teaching and coaching at Manual. Although he had been teaching history at Manual, he had taken no history courses while at the University of Kentucky. Professor Kenneth Vinsel became interested in Ab, and urged him to get a master's degree in history or in political science. However, admission to graduate school would have entailed his earning many undergraduate credits, and Ab felt that he could not invest so much time and energy. After all, he reasoned, his future in football seemed assured. Nevertheless, history intrigued him, and his reading and knowledge of the subject widened rapidly from this time on. In realizing and pursuing this interest, Kirwan had finally stumbled upon his true literary compass point.

Ab's appointment added more fire to an already overheated Male-Manual rivalry. He was hired to beat Male, something the Crimson had achieved only once since 1918. During his six years at Manual, Ab beat Male three times and compiled an overall record of 42 wins, 11 losses, and 2 ties.[20]

For the first time Ab had his own team, and his traits as a coach began to appear. Recruiting was no real problem, for about 200 of Manual's 1,200 boys went out for football; but he was looking for the few who might reveal the same spirit he had shown during his boyhood fights with Martin. One of his former players relates a story that reveals both this appreciation for a fighting spirit and Kirwan's low-key approach. William McCubbin was in Ab's very popular history class at Manual in 1932. One day after class Ab approached this stocky student; he said he'd heard that Bill had thrashed a boy for hitting him with a paper bag full of water. McCubbin admitted he had done so, and then gave his side of the story. Ab casually asked him if he'd ever played football; when told not, he said, "Well, what about coming over to Manual Stadium after class and watching practice?" Young McCubbin agreed. When he arrived, team uniforms were being issued. Coach Kirwan eased up to him, saying, "Bill, you just get in line there if you want one." This gentle approach appealed to the sixteen-year-old; "so I proceeded to get in line like the rest of the boys, . . . and this started my work in athletics with Dr. Kirwan."[21]

Ab never used gimmicks to work up his teams. Here, as everywhere else, he won respect through his genuine efforts to find something good in every person he met. Players wanted to do their best for him; indeed, his interest in them was genuinely warm and paternal. Bill McCubbin also played college ball for Ab, and he remembers that "I could go to him for advice and he would give me some real answers—his judgment was almost like being part of the family." The dressing room scenes were therefore calm and thoughtful; McCubbin recalls: "He would walk and think and always click his heels. All of a sudden he would say, 'We're starting today with - - - ,' and he'd name the players for [each position.] Then he'd remind us of things we'd prepared for for that week, . . . warning us not to be afraid if they do something unusual."

During Kirwan's first season at Manual, heavily favored Male was lucky to eke out a 4-0 win, and this augured well for Crimson fans. The next year, 1933, the great Thanksgiving Day game with Male found Ab's brothers and sisters and 14,000 other wildly cheering fans in the stands as the game went into the fourth quarter with Ab's Crimson team protecting a slim six-point lead. Each team scored two touchdowns in final quarter action "far exceeding" any past meeting of the two teams. Manual's 20-13 victory was only the second over Male since 1918.[22]

It was a proud but exhausted Coach Kirwan who ate his Thanksgiving turkey that evening; indeed, he was doubly proud, for Betty had given birth to their first son, Albert Dennis Kirwan, Jr., on November 29, Thanksgiving eve!

Ab shared the problems of all coaches, but it may not have been coincidental that his 1934 game at Middlesboro came on October 13. Everything went wrong. The team arrived so late Friday evening that they spent the remainder of a sleepless night in their train car. The next morning the team and cheerleaders began pursuing a pig up and down Middlesboro's streets. An angry Ab and his assistant, Ray Baer, entered the chase. The team headed for the tall timber when they saw who was behind them, so Ab and Ray had to hire a taxi to catch them and get them back in time for the game. The foolishness exacted its price in the game, as heavily favored Manual was lucky to escape with a 6-6 tie.[23]

One of Ab's most satisfying wins came the next week at Ashland, whose Tomcats had not lost to a state team in twelve years, and who two years earlier had walloped Manual by 95-0. Several days before the game a heated eligibility squabble developed around Tomcat star Bobby O'Mara. Manual officials discovered that he had been in high school one semester beyond the eight-semester limit set for Kentucky high school athletes. Ab begged the Manual officials to hold back until after the game for fear of further inflaming the powerful Ashland eleven, but they refused and O'Mara was sidelined. Kirwan's widow says that "Ab did not 'do the job' on O'Mara, although the papers and the Ashland fans blamed him."

Manual's team encountered open hostility in Ashland. No transportation awaited them, nor would taxi drivers take them to the distant playing field. Truckers not infected with that week's football fever eventually picked up the hitchhiking players and coaches. Two highly determined teams took the field, but Ab's boys struck for two first-half touchdowns and held on for a 12-7 victory. Paul Jenkins, the Tomcat coach, later went to Louisville's St. Xavier, where he continued his rivalry with Kirwan but never beat him.[24]

Ab finished a memorable 1934 season with a 19-12 victory over Male. Proof of Kirwan's strong hold on the affections of all Louisville fans, whether from Male or from Manual, appeared at the end of this golden anniversary game: "At game's end, 16,000 football fans... stood in salute... to Manual's coach A. D. 'Ab' Kirwan, Male High grid captain... who thirteen years ago led the Purples in a tingling scoreless clash at Old Eclipse Park.... Everything drowned in the salute that went up for 'Ab'. That is, everything but the final touch as 'Ab' extended his hand to the courageous Bill Brown, Male's captain, who filled the same shoes 'Ab' filled thirteen years ago."[25]

During Kirwan's last three years at Manual he steadily built toward his 1938 appointment as coach of Kentucky's Wildcats. He also entered a ten-year rivalry with Wally Butts, who had come to Male in 1935 but moved up to coach the University of Georgia's Bulldogs in 1939. The two high school coaches locked horns on even terms, although an upset win his first year put Butts one game ahead of Ab. They continued their rivalry as college coaches, but Ab was able to win only once, in 1939.[26]

University of Kentucky administrators concluded during the disastrous 1937 season that the head football coach would have to be replaced. Personal problems had caused him to lose control of his team, and even worse, rumors of scandal had circulated when the admittedly powerful Wildcats failed even to score in the six games they lost. Kirwan's widow recalls that "there was dreadful discontent among the players, the families of the players, the faculty, and the townspeople. And the small group who ran athletics (downtown businessmen) were in disgrace for having picked such a disappointing coach."

More was involved, however, than the mere hiring and firing of coaches, for early in 1938 a reorganization was effected in order to bring athletics more fully under the control of the University. Henceforth, coaches were to be faculty members in a new Department of Athletics created in the College of Arts and Sciences, where they would labor under the same privileges and restrictions as other professors. Moreover, an Advisory Council on Athletics was appointed by President McVey from among the faculty and the students. He and the president of the Alumni Association were ex-officio members. In short, the University at this time was not motivated toward winning at all costs, or as Charles Talbert observed, "the new organization did not produce any championship football teams, but criticism from the fans was reduced to a minimum."

Meanwhile, Ab had been approached concerning the coaching job by a former Wildcat star, William "Doc" Rodes, who was then influential in University athletics and Lexington business. According to Betty Kirwan, "in late November 1937, Doc came to Louisville and had dinner with Ab. He wondered if Ab would be interested—but it was all hush-hush because they hadn't fired the other coach as yet. Ab thought he might be—and strangely enough Centre was also looking for a coach and they were making overtures to Ab." Kirwan most wanted to coach at his alma mater; so following the removal of his predecessor he signed a contract in early 1938 as head football coach.[27]

Ab seemed admirably suited to the calm new athletic policy at the University. He was as widely respected for his qualities as a person as he was for his prowess as a coach. Moreover, he was a former gridiron star and alumnus of the University, and he was known and liked by President McVey and many other members of the faculty and administration. For all of these reasons he was hired, and perhaps for those same reasons he was retained until he himself chose to resign seven years later, with a cumulative 23-28-4 record—worse than the 20-19-0 mark left behind by his predecessor.

The Kirwan family moved to Lexington in February 1938, living first on Catalpa Road and then moving to 212 South Ashland Avenue. Later, he and Betty bought a permanent residence at 214 South Hanover Avenue. A few months after coming to the Bluegrass, William English Kirwan, II was born to them on April 14, 1938. He was a redhead destined to pick up the nickname "Brit"—from playmates who teased him about his middle name.

Coach Kirwan's first task was to pick staff members who were both capable and compatible with one another. Bernie Shively, the new athletics director, accepted a staff assignment, as did Frank Moseley, Gene Myers, and Joe Rupert. Although his inexperienced 1938 team beat Maryville and Oglethorpe in the first two games, they lost their seven remaining contests. Perhaps the best one can say for the season is that undefeated Tennessee beat the Wildcats only 46-0 on their way to the Orange Bowl.[28]

The Wildcat athletics program of the 1930s differed greatly in size and approach from the program that followed World War II. There was nothing like the huge athletics fund of the late 1940s. All athletics expenses had to come from the gate receipts generated by the football and basketball teams. "I was always given to understand that all of the expenses of inter-college athletics had to be earned." Queried in 1952 as to the effectiveness of this sytem, Ab replied that he had shown a "very small" profit as coach, and had "never lost any money." He clearly described his program: "We had only sixty scholarships in football at that time, forty varsity and twenty freshmen. We not only broke no rules in awarding grants-in-aid, we did not even grant the full scholarship permitted. We gave only board, room, books and institutional fees at Kentucky at that time. We gave not a cent to any athlete for laundry or for any other purpose."[29]

Ab's great problem in attracting good players to the University of Kentucky is one that still exists— there were relatively few good high school football teams in the state. His marked distaste for recruiting further hurt his chances. "I once or twice took a trip outside the state of Kentucky to talk to high school boys. I didn't like it."[30] Indeed, his widow reveals that "he became disenchanted with coaching when the proselyting became so prevalent. He couldn't bring himself to go around the country begging high school football 'heroes' to come to the University."

The 1939 season was Ab's best at Kentucky. His only losses came from bowl-bound teams. Orange-Bowl-bound Georgia Tech handed the Wildcats their first loss in six games, 13-6. After winning from West Virginia, the Kentuckians turned to meet that great friendly enemy, Tennessee. The winner of this game stood an excellent chance of being invited to the Rose Bowl. Their passing attack brought a 19-0 victory and a trip to Pasadena for the Volunteers, yet Ab was left with a satisfactory 6-2-1 season.[31]

The fine 1939 record led to much optimism among Wildcat fans, an optimism that Kirwan himself did not share. He knew that the conference teams would be ready for him in 1940. They were indeed, and this, along with excessive injuries, brought a disappointing 5-3-2 record. Ab relished a 7-7 tie with Georgia, however, for vaunted "Flatfoot Frankie" Sinkwich was held in check. Ab had recruited Sinkwich the year before, only to have him slip away to Wally Butts's Bulldogs.[32]

Ab fielded his last peacetime team in 1941, recording five wins and four losses. He developed two fine backs in Noah Mullins and Ermal Allen, but the erratic team would often play championship ball one half, and then reverse itself and lose the game in the other.

Two weeks after the locker room closed for the season, Japan attacked Pearl Harbor. Its meaning for college football became clearer the next year.

The 1942 wartime Wildcats dropped to a 3-6-1 record, but Ab could take pride in Clyde "Big Train" Johnson, an Ashland tackle who became the first all-American player in Kentucky's fifty-one years of football. On the same team was center Jay Rhodemyer, destined to step into Johnson's all-American shoes after the war. But now the war began to take precedence over all things. University officials canceled football for 1943, and only four of the twelve SEC schools played a regular schedule that year.[33]

By 1943 the University was moving in a direction that would lead to another career change for Ab Kirwan. On April 16, 1943, the school accepted a War Department contract to train carefully selected soldiers under the Army Specialized Training Program. The purpose was to maintain a pool of college-trained men throughout a war of as yet undetermined length. The first group of soldiers arrived on May 3, and their classes started seven days later. They moved into dormitories, the Phoenix Hotel, and other facilities soon vacated by the remainder of 3,174 army technicians the College of Engineering had trained during the past year.[34]

The sudden surge of student soldiers created near panic in many unprepared departments. History's chairman, Thomas D. Clark, was told on a Saturday to teach 500 soldiers the next Monday—this in addition to the normal student load, when the war had taken most of his professors! "I was in a desperate situation," Clark recalls, "so I sailed through the faculty to see whom I might get to take those classes." During his search he remembered that Professor Charles M. Knapp, a colleague, had often insisted that the football coach be used to teach history. Kirwan and Knapp had long been in the habit of meeting on campus and "talking history." Football coaches ran counter to Clark's grain, but the situation was desperate and perhaps Knapp was right. "So I called him in and talked to him, and told him what we were going to do. He jumped at the idea! He was very, very anxious to take a job like this."[35]

Ab began teaching five sections of freshman history with an enthusiasm that dismayed his colleagues; he was also determined to get his master's degree. Kirwan still lacked sufficient credits in history to gain admission to the University of Louisville Graduate School; so "Kenneth Vinsel of U. of L. let Ab take some history exams and thus get credit, and Tom [Clark] let him take a couple of courses at U.K. for credit so that Ab could make up enough credits to be admitted to the master's program." In the spring of 1944 Kirwan started work on his master's degree, commuting to Louisville each Saturday for classes and talks with Dr. William C. Mallalieu, his adviser, and spending the weekdays teaching at the University of Kentucky. "He really got most of it *in absentia*," recalls Betty Kirwan. On February 24, 1945 he took his master's degree with a thesis entitled, "Cassius Clay's *True American*." He worked hard, but compared to coaching, that "seemed like a breeze."[36]

Kentucky resumed its football schedule in 1944, and Kirwan won two games and lost six during his last season as Wildcat coach. This was one of the few years Kentucky met Tennessee twice, losing by two touchdowns both times. In the final game Kentucky lost to Michigan State by a frustrating 2 to 0 score. Perhaps this was as fitting an end as any for Ab Kirwan's equally frustrating college coaching career.[37]

Ab knew by season's end that he must quit coaching. He was almost forty years old, and he and Betty were planning a new start. However, when Ab handed in his resignation to President Herman Lee Donovan, the peppery executive insisted that he need not resign "as long as I'm president." It was only after considerable effort that Kirwan finally convinced Donovan that he "would never coach another football team." Donovan then pushed himself back in his chair, saying, "All right, now I would like to know how in the world a man like you ever coached football in the first place?"[38] Ab had no answer for that one except to divulge his great love of teaching and his hopes to reenter that field. Donovan was impressed.

Sometime later, Ab walked into the history department office and told Clark that "the only time I've been happy was during these years we have been teaching the ASTP." Clark could "see exactly what was coming": "He told me he was going to give up coaching.... He didn't think he was a very good coach. He wasn't the kind of coach who could compete in the Southeastern Conference—let's put it that way! He wasn't getting any financial support. The Rupp situation was bad—rivalry there among the coaches. He wanted to get out of it ... without getting scarred, and I don't blame him."

Clark heard Ab out, but then told him he lacked the specialized training to fit into the first-rate department planned for Kentucky after the war. Kirwan was crushed until Clark offered to help him get into a doctoral program, promising to hire him once he earned a Ph.D. Ab had no sooner accepted this offer than Clark was on the phone to W. T. LaPrade, the elderly chairman of history at Duke University. LaPrade was glad to hear from his old friend at Kentucky, but he fell into an academic stupor when asked to admit a football coach into his finely geared doctoral program. "Tom," he said, "what in the hell are you trying to do to me—trying to foist a football coach on me?" Clark argued at length, and finally got Ab into the Duke program. One afternoon two years later, after Kirwan had made Phi Beta Kappa, thoroughly impressed the Duke history staff, and won publication of his doctoral dissertation, Clark received a call from LaPrade: "Tom, if you've got any more damn football coaches, send them down to me!"

Meanwhile, Donovan had mulled over Ab's resignation and then called him to his office. He noted that Dean of Men T. T. Jones would retire in 1947, the same year Ab should receive his doctorate. Would Ab like to fill that vacancy upon his return from Duke? Before the startled coach could reply, Donovan offered him a one year's leave of absence at half his coaching salary and promised to recommend him as an associate professor of history when he returned. Furthermore, Donovan continued, a beautiful apartment was included in the plans for a new dormitory (Bowman Hall), for "it is my belief that the dean of men as well as the president should live on campus."[39]

Ab accepted Donovan's proposal and rushed home to tell the good news to Betty and the boys. Football's frustrations were behind the little family, and new horizons ahead. Ab was brimming with confidence and sold the house on Hanover. He was certain he would be back in two years to take over the new dean's apartment in Bowman Hall. That taken care of, a forty-year-old ex-coach, his wife, and two small sons were off for Duke and a life much different from any they had previously known.

Ab's doctoral program at Duke was guided throughout by Charles S. Sydnor, a renowned historian of the American South. Years later, one of Kirwan's books would win a prestigious prize awarded in Sydnor's memory. But now the quality of Ab's thought and writing was beginning to greatly impress Sydnor and such colleagues as Robert Woody. Tangible proof of his progress came on the day Betty answered the phone to hear Sydnor say that Ab had been elected unanimously to Phi Beta Kappa.

However, nothing in the rush of student life could make Ab neglect his family. His boys "have the fondest memories of those two years we spent in Durham. . . . He had a lot of time for us."[40] One evening at supper he happened to guess what Betty was having for dessert. When the boys marveled at this, he said it was really nothing, that he had magical powers over desserts. This started a long running game of "guessing desserts." It got so that the boys would meet him at the bus stop, eagerly waiting to ask him: "What's for dessert tonight?" Ab would immediately pause, place his hand over his head, and say: "I see strawberry shortcake coming—no, no, not strawberry shortcake—I see chocolate pudding. Hmmm, no, is it pudding? Hmmm, no, that's not it. I've got it! I've got it now! It's apple pie!" To this day Betty refuses to tell how he did it. It must be assumed, historians being what they are, that Ab was telling the truth—that he did indeed have "magical powers over desserts"!

The time came for Ab to cap his work with an original and thoroughly researched dissertation. He was convinced he could prove that Mississippi was a microcosm of the post-Reconstruction South in several important ways: Mississippi had done the first and most effective job of recapturing its government from carpetbaggers—and the same could be said of its efforts to deprive the Negro of his political rights. Sydnor approved this thesis, and so Ab entered into some of the hardest sustained work of his life. He had never been to Mississippi, but upon his arrival at the state archives in Jackson, he threw himself into his task with such fervor that the impressed archivist gave him a key to the place. Within a month he had accumulated a massive amount of material, and this, combined with other research notes, enabled him to write a dissertation that not only won him his Ph.D., but gained publication and excellent reviews as his first book: *Revolt of the Rednecks*.[41]

3. DEAN KIRWAN

Shortly after their return from Duke, the Kirwans moved into their new Bowman Hall quarters. And several blocks away, in his Administration Building basement office, Ab was getting used to being called Dean Kirwan. He was located directly under President Donovan, and soon he would become Donovan's right-hand man. The explosive little president, opposed by many as a "nonscholar" when appointed in 1940, had just ended a long fight in gaining a Court of Appeals decision that college teachers did not fall under the $5,000 salary limit placed on state employees by Kentucky's 1890 constitution.[42]

Donovan could be very hard to work with if one were timid or a yes man. Ab was neither. "I know one time we had an issue up," recalls Thomas D. Clark of a committee meeting, "and we were intolerant of Donovan. Ab had the courage to stand up and argue with him, and did so without causing the old man to explode. The old man was just like gunpowder—he would just fly off the handle at nothing! But Ab said, 'You can't do it,' and stood his ground with him. When the chips were down, Ab had courage."

Ab served as dean of men until 1950, at which time he was made dean of students, a post he resigned in 1954. During these seven years his domain expanded mightily, for the flood of veterans increased the student population from 3,000 in 1945 to more than 10,000 just two years later. Donovan built a much larger physical plant, while Kirwan and Dean of Women Sarah B. Holmes met an onslaught of wildly varied student problems. For example, problems were steadily surfacing in Cooperstown and Shawneetown, large housing projects for married veterans. The prefabricated houses were furnished, but the occupants often exchanged furniture according to taste. On one occasion Ab sent out a stern letter to all involved: "These practices must cease." They probably did, for the dean was regarded generally as firm but very fair.[43]

Back at the Bowman Hall apartment, which faced into a quadrangle of men's dormitories, Betty was giving sterling support to her dean. "It was a lovely apartment," she remembers, with two bedrooms and two other rooms that could be used as a guest suite. The family used these rooms in the absence of guests, but at other times "I assumed the responsibility of taking care of the guests, and frequently had them for breakfast and for dinner." President

McVey, then retired, loved to come to these breakfasts and chat.

Betty Kirwan also served as something of a housemother to the multitude of male dormitory residents. She often cured homesickness by inviting the affected lad in to dry the dishes and talk, or perhaps help plan one of the many dances that were held in the Kirwan recreation room.

Some unexplainable urge to vary his walking habits permitted Ab to save a life in 1947. He used to walk out to work behind the Funkhouser Building each morning, passing the "Green Fly" on his way. (This was an appropriately nicknamed student coffeeshop featuring stomach cramps as much as anything else.) For some reason or other, on this particular morning, Ab decided to walk in front of the Funkhouser Building, and in doing so he was irritated to see a car parked up on the front sidewalk. He strode over to scold the driver inside, but before he could open his mouth, the boy said, "Get me some water quick—I've just taken strychnine!"

"When did you take it?" Ab asked calmly.

"Twenty minutes ago," the boy told him. "I walked over behind here and got a Coca Cola. I put it in the Coca Cola and drank it."

Ab did not know whether to give the boy water or not. He ran into the Funkhouser Building and had to force a door to get to a telephone. However, the promised ambulance soon arrived, and Ab accompanied the lad to the hospital, where a stomach pump saved him. Betty Kirwan adds an interesting footnote to the story in that "three years later Ab and I got an invitation to a wedding. The boy had fallen in love and he was getting married." Some things do have a happy ending, even in a dean's life!

Ab's unleashed Irish temper was fearsome to behold. He had great physical strength and of necessity nearly always managed a serene self-control. Occasionally, however, he would be pushed beyond his limits, as is revealed in his handling of a smoking violation in Frazee Hall, where the history department was housed. In spite of personal warnings, "No Smoking" signs, and the fact that the old building had oil-soaked floors, some students persisted in lighting up. One day an admonition to a student by Professor James Hopkins escalated into a furor that ended up in the chairman's office. From there the student was taken before the student government judicial council, tried, and fined ten dollars, payable before he could receive his credits. The last requirement led the lad to a miscalculation that landed him in the dean's office, an encounter he may never forget.

The boy made out a ten-dollar check to the University, but he wrote a long apology on the back so that in endorsing it, the school would be acknowledging his "mistreatment" and apologizing for it. A secretary realized the significance of his act and brought the check to Dean Kirwan. The dean immediately summoned the boy to his office, and asked Clark and Hopkins to be present as well. Clark describes what happened: "The boy gave him some sass in his office. He jumped up and grabbed the boy and slung him literally right through the door and he landed against the wall outside. He ran out and grabbed him up again . . . and hit him against the wall, . . . and the boy said: 'Please, for God's sake, don't throw me again, Dean Kirwan, you'll kill me!' And he would have, I think. And the boy said, 'I'll sign the check and get out of here.' And he did, and that is the first time I knew that Ab could explode."

Years later Ab recalled his days as dean of students during a televised program welcoming President Otis Singletary to the campus. "Some 25 years or so ago I was the Dean of Students. . . . I would certainly be classified as a tyrant. I hope I was a benevolent one, but this was the system. The Dean of Student's authority, insofar as disciplinary matters were concerned—either on the campus or off, made no difference—was supreme. The Dean said 'come' and the student came. He said 'go' and the student went. That time, of course, is gone—long gone—and probably, also, it's well it has. But there has come in place of it a great deal of uncertainty."[44]

Integration came to the University in June 1949. Ab and the dean of women initially interviewed each black student admitted, requesting cooperation in handling the kinds of problems that might arise in an as yet unknown atmosphere. Anticipated trouble failed to develop, however, and Ab was immensely relieved.[45] Another milestone in the maturing University had been resolved in an orderly fashion.

One potential source of trouble on campus was an essentially frivolous bit of pre-60s college pranksterism—the panty raid. One spring evening during the early 1950s the coeds in Jewell Hall began waving their underwear from the windows, enticing an ever-growing throng of males in the street below. Ab and Dean of Women Sarah Holmes were already rushing to counter the affair before someone got hurt. The formidable dean of women had armed herself with a wet floormop, and when one youth attempted to rush up the dormitory stairs, "she wrapped [it] around his head with a flourish." Outside, Ab arrived in a police car with a loudspeaker and ordered the boys to disperse. Some had guns, and he alighted from the car, telling them to "get rid of those guns and go back and quiet down." The students did as he asked.[46]

Ab had a penchant for taking on a job at the worst possible time. He was Kentucky's coach at a time of meager opportunity and little support. He became dean of men when floods of veterans and integration brought unusual and knotty problems. Later he would occupy the graduate dean's chair just as the University faculty were taking sides for or against President John Oswald. Finally, he became president in the midst of student turbulence and even violence. But back in 1948, he wrote a simple acceptance note to Donovan destined to involve him three years later in the nastiest episode of his life—the basketball scandals: "I accept with pleasure the appointment of me as faculty chairman of athletics."[47]

The athletics program Ab was to help administer was already carrying seeds of the overemphasis that would finally wreck it. Donovan later admitted that "the most trying problem of a college administrator is the athletics program," but he had not learned this in 1945, the year he let Frankfort legislators talk him into building "a great football team."[48] (Ab's coaching successor, Bernie Shively, had won only two games that year, losing eight.)

Donovan's program needed money that would be absolutely free of taxes and politics, so he asked for and received contributions from throughout the state to create an independent athletics fund. Within a few weeks, $113,000 was raised and earmarked by the trustees for use by the newly incorporated Athletic Association. This corporation was separate from the University in name only, for Donovan was its president and the eleven members served the University in varying capacities; nevertheless, it had no ties to troublesome tax monies or to even more troublesome alumni. Several years later Judge Saul Streit asked Kirwan if this fund and its manipulation might not mark the beginning of Kentucky's emphasis of athletics, and Ab replied: "That's right."[49] In any event, money was now available to hire Maryland's winning coach, Paul "Bear" Bryant. Truly, the desires of Kentucky's most fervent sports fans had been answered—Rupp and Bryant on the same campus!

Ab's measured return to athletics revived his old sports sense, making him feel as if he were "back in the game." But the "game" had changed considerably the year of his appointment. In 1948, the National Collegiate Athletics Association had adopted the "sanity code," setting up a central agency through which all financial aid to college athletes was now controlled. This meant that the SEC could no longer offer an open grant-in-aid of room, books, board, scholarship, and $15 monthly for incidental expenses, but henceforth offer only tuition and fees. Each athlete had to find work to pay for his own room, board, and incidental expenses. This led almost immediately to the hypocrisy of colleges giving made-up jobs to athletes. Worse, it opened the door for eager businessmen sports fans to provide the players with under-the-table help disguised as "jobs out in town."[50]

By 1950 Kirwan had united with other SEC athletics representatives in a crusade against the sanity code. A southern bloc formed within the body of the NCAA as the Southern and Southwestern conferences joined the SEC in fighting the code. At the 1951 NCAA meeting in Dallas, it was evident that the southern bloc could end the sanity code if it could gain an alliance with the powerful Eastern College Athletics Association. A deal was worked out in which the easterners pledged to vote against the code and the southerners agreed to support retention of the Dartmouth Amendment. Added the year before, this amendment curtailed recruiting by making it unlawful for a school to pay the traveling expenses of prospective athletes to visit member institutions.[51]

Ab's Dallas speech for the SEC against the sanity code brought him national attention. The Nashville *Banner* declared that "it was Ab Kirwan who made the most forceful, the most effective, the most telling speech. He wrote it in longhand on hotel stationery." Ab stood before some 200 balding sports representatives in a hotel ballroom and hammered at the heart of the matter: "If it is not morally wrong to make it possible for a bright student to attend college without working, why is it necessary to penalize his less favorably endowed teammate by requiring him to spend six or more hours a day at a job after his duties in classroom, athletic field, and study have been performed?"[52]

At least one newspaper viewed Ab's speech as "the clincher" in achieving the 130-60 vote that killed the sanity code and retained the Dartmouth Amendment.[53] His impressive appearance in Dallas before this national assembly came at an extremely opportune time for the University of Kentucky. Ab had greatly enhanced his reputation for honesty and courage the very year the basketball scandals horribly besmirched the reputation of his school. The University needed him, and he was ready. At that time, no man in the state could have filled his shoes.

Kentucky's citizens opened their newspapers on October 21, 1951, to read with unbelieving eyes that three players on the 1948-49 basketball team, including two of the "Fabulous Five," had become involved in the nationwide basketball gambling scandals. Bad news led to worse, for the list of Wildcat players implicated eventually included three from the 1949-50 team, one of whom was expected to start in the 1951-52 season about to open. President Donovan reacted by appointing a special committee from the athletics board, of which Kirwan was secretary, to make an exhaustive study of Kentucky's athletics policies and practices. Ab was as surprised as most by the scandal, but his closer connections to it made it more painful. For one thing, one of the involved students had been coaching at his old school, duPont Manual. For another, one of the confessed bribers and a key figure in the team's downfall had earlier played football under him.[54] Finally, Ab had known of widespread underhanded practices in sports for years, and perhaps he felt he might have done more to have prevented the inception of scandal at Kentucky.

By November, rumors flew wildly through Lexington and the state. One concerned the operations of a secret fan club that gave gifts to Wildcat stars for exceptional feats. Since football players were also rewarded by this group, Bryant and his team were drawn into the widening investigation.

Meanwhile, at the urging of Governor Lawrence Wetherby, Vincent A. G. O'Connor, assistant district attorney for New York, came to Kentucky to see how his evidence might fit local information. His subsequent statement convinced the athletics board to suspend the eligibility of the one active player "by reason of the fact that there is evidence tending to show that he is involved in the basketball scandal now under investigation. His eligibility will be reinstated if his innocence is established."[55] Dean Kirwan released this to the press just before Christmas 1951.

To clear himself, the suspended student volunteered in February 1952 to "go to New York, accompanied by a representative of the Board, and testify before the New York Grand Jury, and if after doing so the Board was convinced of his innocence, he would be reinstated." The board commissioned Dean Kirwan to "be present as an impartial observer to all questionings" and to gather all information possible to "throw any light on [the] case and to report back all information to the Board."⁵⁶

After Kirwan had finished his exhaustive study of the records and had talked at length with the litigants and officials, he composed a nine-page report for the athletics board, later entered in the minutes of the board's meeting of March 2, 1952, as an addendum. In this report there is abundant evidence as to why Ab so well filled the exact needs of his University at this moment. His legal training, his athletics experience, and his critical historically trained mind all came into play as he analyzed the situation. New information presented along with Ab's report convinced the board beyond any reasonable doubt that the suspension should be permanent. The next day, March 3, 1952, newspapers carried what Ab fervently hoped would be the last story on his school's basketball misfortunes.⁵⁷

While in New York, Ab testified to aid the basketball investigations of the Court of General Sessions of the County of New York. He appeared before Judge Streit, and the 59-page court report of their question-and-answer interplay clearly reveals Kirwan's philosophy of athletics and their relationship to education. He said that he'd like to do away with athletics scholarships. He believed that college admissions committees should accept only scholastically and academically qualified students, and that athletic ability should have no more bearing on this than musical or typing ability. When a university had granted all the scholarships it could afford, that would be the end of it. Students who wanted to go out for a team and pursue that sport as an academic course could do so; the same thing applied to those students who wanted to involve themselves with the band or theater groups. "That is the way it was when I played," he told Streit, "and I think it was a much better system."⁵⁸

This was not some Johnny-come-lately attitude for Ab. Although he was fully aware that athletics usually paid for its own scholarships, educational processes still took absolute first place. Speaking at a 1940 Frankfort High School football banquet, Coach Kirwan stressed the importance of success in fields other than football, warning that "if you fail scholastically, [then] the things for which you go to school, the things for which schools are built, and the part football plays in all that will be lost to you." Twelve years later, as he fought to save scandal-ridden Kentucky from suspension, he told the SEC executive committee that "it is my personal opinion that athletics are overemphasized at all of our institutions. If I had my way, Kentucky would have given its last athletics scholarship. I think the scholarship is a travesty and a joke. I think it has merely placed a floor under aid to athletes."[59]

Kirwan's session with Judge Streit also revealed his belief that sports contests are relative—football and basketball would be just as entertaining to the fans if colleges had never resorted to costly coaching staffs, huge subsidies, and the recruiting of "all these semipros into a team." He later summed up his lengthy discussion with Streit on this point for the benefit of a Louisville newsman: "I coached for a number of years . . . and I'm confident I couldn't tell the difference in the performance of athletes if two split-second, precision teams were playing or if the third squads of both teams met. Of course, even the average fan can tell the difference if, say, Notre Dame should play Ol' Siwash. But can he tell the difference if two evenly matched teams compete—teams following the same rules insofar as recruiting, subsidization, scholarship and training rules are concerned?" Or, as he told Streit at the time: "When I was in school twenty-five years ago, I was the best player on the football team. I couldn't make [Bear Bryant's present team] if I were that age today. Yet the folks thought we had a good team."[60]

At one point Streit asked Ab this pertinent question: "Can you tell me what you think contributed toward the delinquency of these boys?" Ab's reply was honest. "I have racked my brain. I have talked to them. I have talked with many people about it. I don't know." To blame the lure of money and a high-pressured environment was too simplistic, he said, for most other boys had not succumbed to exactly the same conditions. On the other hand, great teams invariably attract gamblers; perhaps the stars were exposed by their very talents to temptations unknown to run-of-the-mill players. Athletic talent doesn't preclude youth and naiveté, nor favor a boy with any special wisdom to deal with the nature and number of unusual temptations he may have to confront in its service.[61]

A final interesting point emerged from Streit's questioning of Kirwan. The judge wondered about the probable financial loss a university might incur from deemphasizing sports. Ab assured him that this would not happen: "We are no better off now [at Kentucky in 1952] than we were when I was coaching and when our budget never ran as high." Both men then agreed that operating expenses had been permitted to escalate, eating up the profits through excessive travel, staff, recruiting, and surprisingly costly tournament and bowl appearances.[62]

District Attorney Frank S. Hogan recommended leniency for the five Wildcat cagers who had pleaded guilty, and the court gave them suspended sentences. All of the gamblers involved were imprisoned. The sixth student was tried before Judge Streit; the result was a hung jury and the charge was eventually dismissed. With this, Streit issued a 63-page indictment of college sports in general and the University of Kentucky in particular. Although Ab took exception to some of Streit's charges, he admired the judge and believed college sports had long needed just what Streit was giving it.[63]

Worse was coming, for on August 11, the SEC suspended the Wildcat basketball team from conference action during the 1952-53 season. If, as Donovan claimed, Kentucky was being used as a sacrifice to wash away "our common sins," Ab intervened to make it at least worth the effort. In a blazing speech before the SEC executive committee, he drew on his long coaching experience to catalog a most embarrassing list of "common sins" among the personnel and institutions of the conference. Although Donovan called Ab's appeal "one of the most eloquent speeches I have ever heard," the executives stood by their decision. Kentucky would now have to fill out its customary fourteen-game SEC schedule with outside teams such as Wyoming and Minnesota. It was at this point that many Kentucky newsmen began to enlarge upon an alleged statement by Adolph Rupp to the effect that the ban would benefit the Wildcats by giving them the chance to play good teams for a change. This smug speculation did great damage, according to Betty Kirwan, for "it was only then that the NCAA decided to look further into Kentucky's basketball affairs."

The NCAA subcommittee on infractions had been studying Kentucky's athletics program since April at Donovan's request. By November, the NCAA council was ready to make a decision on the case. Ab and University Vice President Leo Chamberlain went to Chicago to present Kentucky's case to the council. Kirwan delivered a speech explaining Kentucky's side of it and pleaded for mercy. That evening Hugh C. Willett, president of the NCAA, invited the two Kentuckians to have dinner with him. Throughout the meal Willett kept telling them that they had made a most wonderful impression on him and the council. Ab's and Leo's hopes soared. But as the meal ended, Willett matter-of-factly added that the council had decided that Kentucky must cancel all of its games for the 1952-53 season! The two stunned Kentuckians immediately took a taxi for the train station, neither saying a word. Finally, Ab turned to Chamberlain, saying, "Leo, has it ever occurred to you what would have happened to us if we hadn't made such a fine impression on the council?"[64]

Kirwan in fact had made a marked effect on the council. Executive Director Walter Byers notified Ab the next year that he had been elected to the subcommittee on infractions. Ab was later appointed chairman of this most important of NCAA committees and served in this capacity until 1960.

Dean Kirwan handled NCAA infractions from his campus office along with his many University duties. With his appointment Kentucky's free-wheeling athletics policies of yore were buried beyond recall. Even before this, the scandals had brought complete faculty control over athletics through a much enlarged representation on the athletics board. As faculty chairman of athletics, Kirwan bluntly told Rupp and Bryant "that in the future all rules must be obeyed by Kentucky, even those [for] which [evasions] are universally condoned." Bryant confessed to Ab that he had broken many rules, but he stated that he would never break another. As was Ab's nature, he never doubted Bryant from then until their relationship ended.[65] Nevertheless, having a powerful NCAA infractions committeeman on the same campus was perhaps more than the aggressive Bryant could bear; in any event, he left Kentucky not long after Ab's appointment. Rupp of course remained. He had been reprimanded for his laxity in handling his team prior to the scandals. Kirwan had lost his respect for Rupp, believing him to have lied to him on at least one occasion during the scandals. Moreover, Ab privately felt that the reason Rupp did not leave Kentucky was simply because he never received any serious job offers elsewhere, possibilities having been dried up by the scandals.[66]

4. THE MATURE LEADER

By 1954 Kirwan was extremely tired and worn from his seven years in the dean's office; he was looking for a reason to change directions again. It came when several Kentucky football players beat up a Lexington policeman. Ab called the players into his office and suspended them after due process, whereupon Donovan probated their sentence. This completely exasperated the tired dean, and when he arrived home, he told Betty that "when you get to this point it is time to quit." And he did, a few days later, reentering the history department. Donovan made him a full professor, and a few years later he inscribed a gift copy of his book, *Keeping the University Free and Growing,* "To A. B. Kirwan, and Betty too. The best dean of men ever." Donovan, like so many others, was never able to untangle Ab's nickname from his initials.

Ab returned to teaching in the fall of 1954, and he was midway through his second semester in March 1955 when the intense strain and tension of the past few years overtook his heart. The attack caused no pain and was typical of attacks to come in 1966 and finally in 1971. Although he took no medicine, he was in bed for some time and had to learn to slow down; however, he was not forced to change his life or character radically. Indeed, that September he went back to teaching one class and gradually built up to a full schedule.

Kirwan's courses on the South, the Civil War, and various surveys were always packed with students. Thomas D. Clark assesses his popularity this way: "If you set out to determine what makes a good teacher, you would, I think, discover these things about Ab: . . . Number one, he had a good voice, and he was willing to lift it up so the students could hear what he was saying. Second thing, he was experienced enough on his feet that he could handle anything that came up in the average class. [Third,] he handled his subject with a great deal of certainty. [Finally,] he had a very rich, warm personality, and the students loved him for that. He was a very popular teacher."

A former student probably summed up the matter when he said, "I sensed that Dr. Kirwan was teaching people and not just subject matter." Another student recalls that when he went to Kirwan's office, "he made me feel that I was as important as a corporation executive." One of Ab's graduate students remembers that "he always left his door open, and I could hear him (because my office was so close) talk to numerous student advisees, and he treated each one as an individual case. . . . He even had time for the students that weren't working under him."[6][7]

Ab's teaching popularity was not based on his being an "easy grader." Indeed, his warm personality lulled many a student into a false sense of security prior to the first test. Professor Hopkins touches on this in recalling that "as a colleague, he was as easy to work with as anybody I know. I think the students found him easy to work with, although he was pretty exacting. Once he and I conducted a seminar together, and I was a little surprised to find that his standards were very high, and he would not budge from them. I mean I had become accustomed to the easygoing [side of the] man."[68] In any case, students flocked to his courses, in spite of the quantity—and probably because of the quality—of the work he expected of them. Moreover, he was genuinely interested in them, and their response indicates that this is what counted: in 1966 the student body elected him to receive the Great Teacher Award.

In 1970, as he neared the end of his career, Ab set down his ideas concerning good college teaching. "It is relatively easy to measure faculty competence in research; it is more difficult to measure quality in teaching. I believe that more often than not the good teacher is a productive researcher, and *vice versa*." Experience had also taught him that a reasonable teaching load need not be sacrificed in order to maintain quality research. "In bygone days I taught two large classes (forty or more students each) every semester and in two of every three summer semesters while at the same time keeping office hours in an administrative post. At the same time I was able to maintain a consistent research program. . . . I believe almost any professor in an academic area should be able to teach three courses each semester."[69]

Kirwan, as any great teacher, taught his students much more than the details of his subject or specialty. The student newspaper, often a thorn in the side of University administrators, reveals this in an editorial following Ab's death. "He was responsible, hard-working, enthusiastic, and made few enemies. He believed in his country, and worked selflessly to defend what he determined to be in the better interest of his fellows. Some may criticize such traits today, but after considering the record of such a human as Kirwan, it seems more difficult. He received recognition not only from his academic colleagues; students nominated him for high honors almost as often, and these honors were not unmerited.... His phrases were not hollow platitudes.... The University of Kentucky will miss his presence."[70]

Ab's parting advice to graduate students leaving to take their first posts as college teachers always contained a humorous admonishment to "avoid committee work like a plague." This invariably brought laughs, for his students knew that he was not practicing what he preached. Committee work was so much a part of Kirwan's academic life that it might be well to reveal his assignments over a two-year period, 1966-1967. During this time he was chairman of the following University-wide groups or committees: graduate council, graduate scholarships and fellowships, faculty research, faculty summer fellowships, and large equipment research fund. He served as a committeeman on the University of Kentucky Research Foundation and on the University Press, and he was a member of the athletics board of directors. He served his college and department on the arts and sciences council, the arts and sciences committee to advise the dean in faculty achievement criteria, and was chairman of the history department committee to review fields and areas. He also served on numerous presidential ad hoc committees. His committee work did not end at campus boundaries, but extended into Lexington and surrounding states. He was president of the Central Kentucky Concert and Lecture Association and chairman of the Lexington Public Library board. Moreover, he served as a consultant to Miami and Ohio universities on the advisability of inaugurating doctoral programs in history. Finally, he was chairman of the National Collegiate Athletics Association committee to award graduate fellowships, and he also sat on the long-range planning committee for the same organization. In spite of all this, and perhaps amazingly, these were not only his last two years as graduate dean, but the period during which he returned to full-time teaching, and coauthored a 438-page book, *The South since Appomattox*. It is not surprising, therefore, that he received the highest possible rating for his work during 1966 and 1967 in the College of Arts and Sciences' "Annual Evaluation of Faculty Achievement." Considering Ab's classroom performance, public service, committee work, and scholarly production, the dean commented, "one can hardly point to growth in one who has grown completely, but a full rating of 4 is close to the mark and is definitely justified."[71]

Kirwan's success as a human being issued from a balanced and likable personality. Carl Cone, Ab's chairman in the history department from 1965 to 1970, maintains that "he had more close friends than anybody I think I have ever known." Albert Tanner, the boy who had watched games from Ab's Sigma Nu window, and later served Ab and several other presidents as butler at Maxwell Place, knew Kirwan for fifty years in varying capacities; yet he easily remembers that "I never heard him say anything against anybody. He was one of the kindest and gentlest men I have ever met—always willing to help somebody." A man on Ab's teams of the 1930s insists that "one of the great characteristics of Ab Kirwan was that no matter where you met him after you played football for him, and no matter what your status of life, he always knew you and was glad to see you."[72] On the other hand, Brit Kirwan points up a paradox concerning his father: "I guess to a number of people who didn't know Dad very well, he could perhaps give the impression of being extremely tough, and he was tough if he made up his mind about something; he just wasn't going to budge from it, and he could be as tough as they come."

A very dependable and delightful part of Ab Kirwan was his sense of humor. He easily laughed at himself, telling stories of humorous episodes in his own life rather than jokes "making the rounds." However, his humor could also accommodate itself to almost any occasion. Thomas D. Clark, no mean storyman in his own right, illustrates this ability:

> Ab got up to speak ... and he saw that there was somebody there that was going to embarrass him, that knew a whale of a lot more about what he was going to talk about than he knew. He therefore told the story of the old man who had lived in Johnstown, Pennsylvania, and had gone to Heaven. He had just bored everybody to death on earth telling the story of the Johnstown Flood. And when he got to the gate of Heaven, he was telling St. Peter of the Johnstown Flood, and St. Peter said: "That's all right, you can go ahead and tell me, but I want to warn you, if you tell anybody else around here, Noah will be in the crowd."

Perhaps Ab's greatest asset was his marriage to Betty Heil. As a close friend put it, "If there ever was a perfect match, there's one. . . . Betty was the great love of his life, and she complemented him in every way." A graduate student recalls being introduced by Ab and Betty to several noted historians at a 1970 convention party. Typically, Ab draped his arm over his student's shoulder and warmly presented him. "Dr. Kirwan's wife said something that was humorous. Then she said, 'Oh, excuse me, dear; maybe I embarrassed you.' He said, 'Darling, you couldn't say anything that would embarrass me.' "[73]

Ab and Betty did everything together. She attended all of the meetings and conventions with him—"I always went along because, well, I always went along whenever he went to anything." And each one supported the other in the vast amount of entertaining required by Ab's various high positions at the University and his constant immersion in Lexington community projects. It would be difficult to exaggerate Betty's warmth and grace as a hostess, or her ability as a conversationalist. Whether Ab was carefully concocting one of his justly famous old-fashioneds for the guests, or Betty was discussing the progress of research on the latest book, they did it with a flair, with charm, but above all with one another. After Ab's heart attack, Betty began going with him when he walked for exercise. He walked two miles to school and back each day. Betty always met him on the way home, and the couple became a familiar sight to residents along the way, "the two of them meeting and walking home together holding hands."[74]

Home for Ab and Betty meant a rambling buff brick house at 535 Russell Avenue. The family had moved there in 1954 upon surrendering the campus apartment after Ab's resignation as dean of students. Built in 1914, its quiet two-storied presence sits comfortably among neighboring homes along the heavily shaded street. To the front is Bell House, surrounded by several acres of tree-studded parkland bedecked each spring with redbud, magnolia, and dogwood. The house and its small lawn profit greatly from this setting. The spacious interior, with high ceilings, a solarium in the front, and family room at the rear, reflects solid comfort. And if the house mirrored Ab's likings, so did the nearby part of Lexington still known as "Ashland," the former estate of Henry Clay. A ten-minute walk to the southeast, and Ab could stand on Clay's doorstep or stroll at length in "Old Harry's" formal garden.

The Kirwans reared and disciplined their two sons in a manner that produced harmony in the household. "My entire recollection of my childhood," says Denny, "was that Mom and Dad didn't act singly, they always acted as a team." Moreover, they "took into consideration my own natural characteristics, and their approach with Brit took into account his characteristics." Denny, for example, had to learn things the hard way, and it took the direct approach to convince him. Brit, by contrast, could be cajoled or teased into behaving. A sensitive child, Brit could be crushed by the admonishing clap of his father's hands. Reason, however, usually prevailed, and there was very little use of either spanking or handclapping. Yet, Ab's brother Will notes that Ab had the time to reason with his boys, a luxury that their own father did not always have with the large family back in The Point.[75] This may have made time spent with his children all the more valuable to Ab.

Kirwan never pushed his boys to play football, but he was glad when they chose to do so. By midautumn of 1948, Denny was showing great promise on Coach John Heber's Henry Clay High School Blue Devils. Then, for no apparent reason he started faltering, and in the Irvine game his position was overrun almost at will. Unfortunately, the next day revealed that there was much more wrong with him than his blocking, and he was rushed to the hospital.

At the hospital Drs. Ralph Angelucci and Grandison McLean made spinal tests and then reported to Ab and Betty that Denny had contracted poliomyelitis. "Shall we go in the room and tell him?" they asked the parents. Ab said, "No, I want to tell him." Denny's parents walked across the hall and into his room, and Ab said, "Old boy, I've got some bad news for you—you've got polio." Denny replied with a wry smile: "Well, that will make me immune for life, won't it, Dad?" Fortunately his case proved mild, and he left the St. Joseph Hospital isolation ward that December, continuing his therapy at home. His recovery was complete, and the next year he was back on the Blue Devil football squad.[76]

Betty Kirwan still treasures a theme written by Brit in 1956 for his high school English class. It reveals clearly the relationship that existed between Ab and his sons, and is entitled, "The Most Admirable Person I Ever Met."

> In the community in which I reside a nightly event has come to mean very much to all my neighbors. This event, though small and unimportant, is one that almost everyone looks forward to. Around seven o'clock each evening the

figure of a man, swinging his hickory walking cane, may be seen strolling up the walk. Accompanying this man is his small dog. The reason this event has become so meaningful is relatively simple. My character has always some kind word or interesting bit to say to every person along his route. This may hardly seem enough to base a theme on, but the qualities of this man go much deeper.

He was reared in a large family, and as the strongest and most popular, received the largest portion of the daily chores. This bothered him not, and he was always ready to lay down his work to help a brother or sister who was in distress.

This desire to help others has carried on into later life, and although he is often confronted with immense problems, no one has a problem too small to receive his aid. He always thinks of others first, invariably placing himself last and least important. In spite of having received the highest awards he still retains a humble attitude which makes him popular with people in all walks of life.

In his unusually difficult life he always keeps a fresh attitude, and is ready to tackle any problem with his greatest effort and enthusiasm.

I spoke earlier of his accomplishments and I would like to list a few of them to show that I am not the only one who admires this man. In athletics he always captained the team and was an inevitable choice on the all-star teams. He also excelled in scholastic work receiving excellent marks in school. Upon graduating from college he received his Master's and Ph.D. degrees. His work on his Ph.D. was so outstanding that he was a unanimous choice for Phi Beta Kappa, the highest scholastic honor anyone can receive. He has written three books and is a full professor at the University of Kentucky.

As a result of his overly busy and difficult life he suffered a severe heart attack last spring. But even death itself was not great enough to conquer him. Fighting back from the very doors of death he has almost made a complete recovery. Even in his convalescence he has excelled. He completed another book, and still more important, has become the neighborhood idol.

Ask anyone and he will tell you, "Ab Kirwan is the most admirable person I ever met."

Few weeks passed without social activity at the Kirwan home. Ab was a "great entertainer," and Betty "was just the best at it." Kirwan was president of the Central Kentucky Concert and Lecture Association, and many celebrities dropped by for post-concert parties. Then there was a multitude of local friends to honor with parties. These home events were not always limited in size, for the entire history department came with their wives for dinner once a year. Not infrequently, forty or fifty students were invited for "supper." When the new president and his family, the Otis A. Singletarys, came to the University, the Kirwans introduced them to the Bluegrass and to alumni all over the state with a party to which four hundred were invited. Whether the party was large or small, Ab and Betty enjoyed entertaining people. On the other hand, they "were always on the preferred list when somebody was having a party. They were great company."[77]

Ab took on still another role during the last fifteen years of his life—that of a doting grandfather. Denny married Delia Link, a professor's daughter, in 1956, and over the next five years Ab and Betty became the delighted grandparents of three boys—Michael, Patrick, and Albert. By this time Brit had married Patricia Harper, a Lexington girl he had known since junior high school days. Soon Ab and Betty had another grandson, Patrick, and their first granddaughter, Ann Elizabeth. Until Ann arrived, it had been a man's world for Betty, who had reared two sons and then watched the steady arrival of grandsons.

Over the years Ab had developed a small bald spot, which was soon discovered by his tiny grandsons as they clambered around on him. "Where did that come from, Granddaddy?" They knew very well where it had come from, for they always asked the same question and thereby got Ab to continue his stories of hunting with Daniel Boone. Ab and Boone, it seemed, were old friends, and it would be hard to say which one was the greater hunter. One time when they were out on a long hunt, the Indians attacked and got away with part of Ab's scalp. At this point in the story, little eyes widened with awe and reverence, for the evidence was right there before them to be seen and touched and greatly admired. This was indeed a bald spot of which anyone could be proud![78]

Albert D. Kirwan's name appeared on the title pages of six books as either author or editor. His writing style reflected his personality in its comfortable yet concise simplicity. He loved to write, for the act itself represented the fruit of painstaking research. He wrote, therefore, with a kind of intense persuasiveness and seemingly effortless command of fact about every facet of his various subjects. His doctoral dissertation, for example, was so well wrought that it was published, "changing only the first chapter to the third and the third to the first," as *The Revolt of the Rednecks,* a 328-page book, in 1951 by the University of Kentucky Press. Reviewer Rupert Vance hailed it as a "surprisingly calm and objective study of the fifty-year struggle of the Woolhat boys and the rednecks to gain and to hold control of the Democratic party of Mississippi." C. Vann Woodward, a renowned historian of the South, credited Ab's originality and praised the book as "an outstanding contribution to...recent American political history." Ab later revealed that this study of Mississippi had taught him "that culture, progressive ideas, and liberalism are not apt to flourish in a rural society as much as in an urban society, Thomas Jefferson, to the contrary, notwithstanding."

Although Ab wrote from a liberal stance, Francis B. Simkins's review emphasized that Kirwan was "no bigoted liberal attempting to impose an imported code of civic rectitude upon a benighted commonwealth of the Deep South. Like William Faulkner he finds virtues in Mississippi characters of both good and bad repute, with a partiality for those the civic prudes call bad." In contrast, a grandson of one of the politicians Ab handled in the book wrote a reviewer that "Professor Kirwan belongs to that group of neo-liberals, which we now have in this country, who believe in the 'handout and welfare state.'" The excellent reviews elated Ab and Betty, for it must be said that the two of them worked as a team in this as in everything else, with Betty contributing talented criticism, research time, and typing.[79]

The dean's desk and the athletics scandals forced Ab to lay his pen aside until 1955. Early that year Thomas D. Clark and Bruce F. Denbo, director of the University Press, obtained the Civil War diary of Louisvillian John W. Green. Green had joined with fellow Kentuckians in 1861 to form a Confederate brigade, but when Kentucky remained in the Union the unit was nicknamed "the Orphan Brigade." Ab accepted Clark's and Denbo's offer to edit the diary, and he set about dividing the narrative and supplying pertinent information. His heart attack stopped him temporarily, but he was soon happily and healthfully checking galley proofs. The 217-page book was published in 1956 as *Johnny Green of the Orphan Brigade: The Journal of a Confederate Soldier*. It arrived as the nation moved toward its Civil War centennial and became one of the Press's best-selling books. Reviewer Herbert Weaver denoted its appeal when he wrote that "the contents of the journal plus the fine editorial work make this a delightfully readable volume."[80]

By 1959 the ever-widening Civil War centennial market beckoned publishers. World Book planned a series of books called Meridian Documents of American History; the first was to be a comprehensive but nonmilitary collection of the principal documents of the Confederacy. When consulted regarding this, Thomas D. Clark suggested Kirwan for the editing job, and Ab accepted. He and Betty traveled throughout the South picking material from numerous collections. His plan was to explore topically the social, cultural, political, economic, and diplomatic aspects of life in the Confederate states. He adhered to a chronology within each topic, choosing 150 pieces of contemporary writings to fill out a picture of all facets of life in the beleaguered South. Each was linked to each by a very readable narrative. *The Confederacy* was published in 1959, and shortly thereafter a reviewer glowingly reported that Kirwan "has brought skill, experience and imagination to bear on his task, for this is no perfunctory collection of obvious documents."[81] It also appeared as a 320-page paperback on commercial bookracks, becoming the best-selling book Ab ever wrote.

Three years after the publication of *The Confederacy*, Kirwan brought out his fourth book, *John J. Crittenden: The Struggle for the Union*. Seldom have a man and his biographer been so perfectly matched as Crittenden and Kirwan. Ab's description of the gentle Crittenden as a man of "great simplicity" and "high integrity" can be applied equally to Kirwan himself. Ab loved his subject, and this became his best book, proving him a mature scholar. He wrote it in 1960-61 while on leave as a Guggenheim Fellow. Something of Ab's love of his subject—and of his relationship with his wife as well—are revealed in a letter that he wrote to Thomas D. Clark in July 1962: "Betty and I are working every spare minute we can find putting the finishing touches on 'Old Crit.' We hope to have the finished manuscript in [the editor's] hands in the next two weeks, although I still have considerable fat-boiling to do. Poor Betty works all day checking footnotes while I am at the office, and then works far into the night with me proofreading and giving editorial advice. Her judgement is good."

Kirwan filled an important biographical gap with this 514-page volume. John Jordan Crittenden served in many high government posts, but his most notable effort was the famous Crittenden Compromise offered a few days before the secession of South Carolina. This was a collection of unamendable constitutional amendments and congressional resolutions designed to placate each section and thereby save the Union. Here Kirwan dropped his historical axe on the Republicans, concluding that they "slaughtered every meaningful compromise" in the dying moments of the old Union. Ab's mastery of his subject won the universal admiration of reviewers. Roy F. Nichols praised the way a massive amount of material had been handled without in any way marring Crittenden's image, concluding that Kirwan's "portrait of the man can be called definitive." Indiana's Robert G. Gunderson spoke of "this definitive biography" in asserting that "at last there is a biography worthy of John J. Crittenden."[82]

The superb reviews foretold many honors for Kirwan. His departmental colleagues voted him the Hallam Book Award. He then won the Alumni Faculty Award for 1962-63. The next year the Southern Historical Association selected *Crittenden* as winner of the Charles S. Sydnor prize for the best book on Southern history published in 1962-1964. He was the first of Sydnor's former students to win this prestigious honor. Betty phoned the news to him while he was attending an NCAA meeting in California. He told her later that he was so pleased he "never went to sleep all night."[83]

Meanwhile, Thomas Clark had come under contract to Oxford University Press to do a book on the South since the Civil War. He invited Ab to be co-author. Their 438-page work appeared in 1967 as *The South since Appomattox: A Century of Regional Change*. This was the first of Ab's books to receive mixed reviews. Carl N. Degler, an eminent historian, hailed it as "an admirable synthesis," praising its handling of social and economic themes, and believed it "ideal for adoption in Southern History classes." Rice Estes held that the book's coverage of the "period from Truman to Johnson" was its greatest strength, while another reviewer expressed exactly the opposite viewpoint. All reviewers, however, believed that the book exploded many old myths, and Ab's "excellent chapter" on

Populism garnered much praise. On the other hand, most reviewers agreed with Joseph F. Steelman that "this study is flawed by too many careless and trifling errors of fact."[84]

Ab's last book, *The Civilization of the Old South: Writings of Clement Eaton,* appeared in 1968. Kirwan edited these writings as a tribute prior to Eaton's retirement from the University history department in 1968. Following an introductory essay, Ab chose thirteen chapters from Eaton's previously published studies of the Old South. Reviewer Thomas P. Govan believed the chosen chapters adequately explained Eaton's contention that the South's problems arose from an "intellectual blockade" which shut out new ideas after 1828.[85] Meanwhile, Kirwan had already turned from this small project to what he hoped would be a sequel to his Crittenden book—a major new study of Henry Clay.

Several paths had led Kirwan to a great interest in Henry Clay. Along with his work on Clay's lieutenant, Crittenden, he had become involved in the University's long-range project to edit and publish *The Papers of Henry Clay*. In 1968, despite the great amount of committee work he was already doing, he agreed to chair the five-member Commission on the Clay Papers. Editor James Hopkins reveals that of several such appointees, "Ab is the only one . . . who really took his job seriously and did things to help us. . . . He went out of his way to help in getting National Historical Commission approval for grants to the Clay Papers."[86]

One other effort of Kirwan's in the publishing field must be noted. He had long shown great interest in the University of Kentucky Press; indeed, four of his six books were done through this publisher. In 1967, when Thomas D. Clark, chairman of the Press committee, learned that other state colleges were planning to set up on-campus presses, he proposed a cooperative press—a consortium of state institutions drawn up in equal rank within the University of Kentucky Press. Such a cooperative press, organized under a meaningful new name, The University Press of Kentucky, would be assured an increase in the flow of Kentucky manuscripts to be published, and at the same time, prevent destructive institutional competition for state publishing funds.[87]

Clark's idea seemed sound, but it could have sunk on the shoals of traditional intrastate collegiate rivalries. Ab's statewide image and prestige were helpful here, for he was able to lend weight to the proposal and provide a common point of reference for the various types of persons who would comprise the consortium. He accompanied Clark to the final meeting at Eastern Kentucky University in 1968, and was "influential in getting over the last hump"—that of getting a nine-university agreement on the consortium. Shortly after this, Clark retired, and Kirwan succeeded him as chairman of the Press committee. In reviewing the years since then, Bruce Denbo concludes that "Ab's contributions were of terrific value in helping to cement a relationship which Clark had so expertly begun."[88]

By 1960 Ab's administrative talent had lain idle for six years. He was delighted when President Frank Dickey offered him the Graduate School deanship, but told him that he had applied for a prestigious Guggenheim Fellowship, and if awarded it, he would have to have a year's leave. Dickey accepted this stipulation. Ab and another member of the history department received Guggenheims, the first ever to be awarded to active members of the Kentucky faculty. Kirwan therefore took a year's leave of absence before actually serving as graduate dean. Meanwhile, Tom Clark had philosophically accepted this most recent loss of Kirwan from his staff: "I told him, 'Now I've gotten you out of the football situation, I've gotten you out of the Dean of Men's situation, and now you're right back in the middle of it as Dean of the Graduate School.' Ab seemed to me to have a real yen for administrative work. He seemed to have been a man who depended on it. It did something for his ego to have that kind of a job. He wouldn't have admitted that to himself, but I'm sure that that was true."[89]

Kirwan's elevation to the summit position of deanships irked no small number of the faculty. No one knew what was going on until the appointment was announced.[90] The present graduate dean, Wimberly Royster, recalls several professors saying, "Oh my! . . . Here's a man who's been football coach, dean of men, and wandered around here from pillar to post, so we're getting another fellow who really doesn't know what a university is all about."[91] Ab had stepped into another unusually difficult job, one in which his performance would be closely and even jealously watched. And a further complication was to arise when a new president split the school into quarreling factions. Kirwan's countertalent for choosing the worst possible time to take new jobs had certainly not failed him here.

Kirwan entered his new job with accustomed grace and ease, yet he was determined to develop a quality graduate program. He chose Lewis Cochran as his associate dean, believing him to know "where quality was and ... was not" among the faculty.[92] Cochran, who has continued to serve the University in various high posts, recalls that "Ab was for research and for quality in the student body and in the faculty. He had aspirations for the University to grow and develop in those directions, and he worked hard to bring it about."[93]

Kirwan emerged as an academic statesman during his eight years as graduate dean. He served his University's scholarly needs better from this office than from any other he ever held. Indeed, Kirwan so rebuilt the Graduate School that one can say he laid much of the foundation of quality from which the modern University continues to rise. He was of course fortunate in serving under two presidents who understood what a university ought to be, and agreed to his proposals.

Ab realized that his new office lacked meaningful authority and as it was could exert little significant institutional influence. Until this was changed, his job would be largely a mechanical one of keeping graduate students' records, determining eligibility for graduation, and checking courses in the curricula with the graduate council. A good indication of the graduate dean's traditional status—and of the task to which Ab had set himself—was the fact that the very admissions to the Graduate School were controlled not by Ab, but by the Registrar's office! One of Kirwan's first moves was to have graduate admissions placed under his authority. This was a hopeful beginning, and additional support soon followed.

Early in 1963 the University Faculty, a representative body elected from the faculty at large, adopted a special committee report recommending that Dean Kirwan be given additional powers. President Dickey quickly implemented the report, giving Kirwan the power to make recommendations on faculty appointments, tenure, and budgets insofar as these items affected the Graduate School. Dickey observed that "the dean was consulted informally on these matters in the past, but now it will be on an official basis."[94] In any event, Ab could now begin to influence some of the factors that determine a high standard of graduate work.

Ab's life at home and at work was especially satisfying to him by 1963. Upon his appointment as graduate dean, he resigned as chairman of the NCAA infractions committee. Not wanting to lose him entirely, however, Walter Byers appointed Ab chairman of the graduate fellowship committee. Ab enjoyed this, for it entailed awarding hundreds of one-year graduate fellowships to athletes who had superior academic records. He also kept his ties with the history department, teaching one class each session. During his first two years in the graduate office he wrote his fine *Crittenden*. All of his talents were happily employed; yet even as he worked, the curtain was closing over the academic serenity that had so long endured on the Bluegrass campus. Frank G. Dickey resigned as president, and two months later, on September 1, 1963, John W. Oswald was installed in that office.[95]

The interim period between Dickey's resignation and Oswald's arrival provided Ab with his first major opportunity to improve the graduate program. A. D. Albright was serving as interim executive. Kirwan's associate dean recalls that "Ab participated very effectively in the making of the internal budget during the transition period . . . I thought it was one of the best budgets the University had to that time. We felt that academic needs were given proper representation."

Ab had been granted substantial powers of appointment, tenure and budgeting under Dickey, yet they were hard to bring to bear against suspicious deans, institutional inertia, and members of the faculty who for various reasons had little enthusiasm for the development of scholarship at the University. While Kirwan pondered this situation, President Oswald did something about it by implementing the recommendations of the University Faculty. Although this greatly enhanced Ab's power and program in the Graduate School, it also unleashed terrific campus dissension.

The new policies and procedures called for term appointments of deans and departmental chairmen, and for the periodic review and evaluation of these academic officers. Another provision created the Academic Area Advisory committees, thus involving the faculty in appointments and promotions. Significant changes were also made in tenure policy. Finally, policy and procedures were established to determine merit salary increases based on an annual performance review of each faculty member. In implementing these new procedures, Oswald abruptly removed and replaced several deans, an act, that brought about heated debate and polarization of campus sentiment regarding administrative policy.[96] Indeed, two of the deans removed had graduated with Ab in the class of 1926. This was ironic, but Kirwan believed their colleges "were in bad shape," and "he could see no other remedy."[97] Although Ab often advised against Oswald's slashing means to gain his ends, he too was unyielding whenever confronted with a clear choice between his ideas of academic excellence and what he considered to be even partial incompetence, and he was no respecter of persons in such matters.[98]

One of Kirwan's greatest needs was for money to finance fellowships and thus strengthen the graduate program. Unexpected new sources of money became available as the Vietnam war escalated, bringing with it increased government research grants. At the same time there arrived shoals of new students born during the "baby boom" following World War II. Ab welcomed the new money, but he also welcomed the opportunity to hire quality faculty to serve the rapidly expanding enrollment. These were exciting years for a dean who could remember Kentucky only as a "have not" institution. Up until this time very few non-service graduate fellowships had been available. The University had been offering about twenty such awards each year, mostly from Kentucky Research Foundation grants, allocations from the Haggin Trust, and occasional private gifts. Additional funds mounted rapidly with the passage of the National Defense Education Act, and the establishment of institutional awards programs for the support of graduate students by the National Science Foundation and the National Aeronautics and Space Authority. These grants, and others, soon amounted to almost $1,000,000 annually, permitting the award of about 175 non-service fellowships each year, and thereby contributing greatly to the growth and quality of the Graduate School. Ab, however, was able to increase his share of this amount by as much as $350,000 annually because Oswald permitted the Graduate School to keep all of the "cost-of-education-allowances" ($2,500 to $3,000 annually) that came with each national fellowship. Instead of dividing each allowance between the Fellow's department, the Graduate School, and the University, it was all given to the graduate dean to use in the development of research and in the improvement of graduate education programs. Graduate deans elsewhere were seldom able to obtain so much of such funds for their programs.

Ab quickly placed this money at the service of scholarship. He established a $50,000 fund to support the travel of professors reading papers at national meetings. The faculty research fund was enlarged from an insignificant amount to about $80,000 annually, and provided research grants to professors in the humanities and other areas that were without strong federal funding. Another beginning in which he participated was made in 1964 when Summer Faculty Research Fellowships of $1,200 each were awarded to 125 University teachers. This especially aided younger faculty members in providing them with time and funds to get their research started. Kirwan's deep interest in the doctoral program led to the start of the dissertation fellowship awards. Financial support was provided for doctoral candidates who had passed their qualifying examinations, thus giving them the opportunity to complete their dissertations and take their doctorates before leaving the University.[99]

Another significant development was Ab's appointment as executive director of the University of Kentucky Research Foundation. (Earlier known as the Kentucky Research Foundation, it was chartered as a non-profit corporation in 1945 by members of the faculty, administration and trustees of the University. It has broad authority to conduct and manage research and to serve as the agent of the University for the administration of extramurally funded grants and contracts.) As executive director, Ab was able to influence the scholarly research programs of the institution, and this period is marked by a substantial growth in extramural funds and scholarly publications.

Another of Oswald's moves extending Ab's influence was the creation of the academic council. This was a work-group of the highest University officials which met every two weeks, usually at Carnahan House for an informal and relaxed discussion and analysis of University operations. Here was a unique opportunity for Ab; as a member of this council, he was able to help direct the policy of the University, and to make his case for graduate education and scholarship. In this he had the agreement and support of President Oswald.

By 1965 the graduate dean had emerged with a much more influential and prominent institutional role. He was steadily obtaining more money, and Oswald had brought him very much into the evaluative process with respect to the appointment and promotion of faculty. He was now in a position powerful enough to develop the academic quality of the University. His associate dean believes that from here on "he truly played the role of academic statesman."

Ab made the most of this opportunity to promote quality throughout the University. He had won much respect, albeit grudging at times, in various parts of the school, and his relationship with President Oswald was such that "he was able to exercise great influence on appointment, promotions, and retentions. This led to some very seriously strained relations with some segments of the University community."

Kirwan did "strain relations" in effecting change, but this issued in part from the emphasis some of the University's colleges had historically placed on undergraduate education. Ab's belief that scholarly research and publication improved undergraduate teaching was not universally shared, and indeed, some scorned it as "publish or perish." In addition, Ab's tendency to back professors in projects that seemed worthy to him but did not receive departmental support was sometimes attacked as meddling. Another source of friction was his determination to hire or promote only quality men. On one occasion, Kirwan recommended against the appointment of several nominees for departmental chairman and triggered complex and divisive problems of long duration thereby.[100] Here, as always, Kirwan carefully studied each situation before making up his mind, but once his mind was made up he became immovable.

As his purpose became clearer, Dean Kirwan did make many new friends around campus, particularly among the younger faculty. Donald Leigh joined the Engineering College in 1965, one reason being that "I was very impressed ... meeting Kirwan ... when I came here for my interview." The onetime engineering student "treated engineering very well," says Leigh. "We had quite a lot of interaction with him as we started our graduate program in the Department of Engineering Mechanics.... I think he ... was taking definite steps to try and strengthen engineering."[101] Other colleges were receiving similar attention from the graduate dean, yet there were blind spots in Ab's overall view of his program.

Kirwan was a scholar and researcher in the basic discipline of history. This somewhat dimmed his understanding of and appreciation for post-baccalaureate or professionally oriented programs such as nursing, social work, home economics and other programs that by their nature did not then closely resemble research-based graduate education. "He didn't have much patience or regard for those," recalls a colleague; "the scholarship wasn't there, the research wasn't there, and yet these programs are a very necessary part of a public university's operation."

When Ab left the dean's office in 1966 to become a Fulbright lecturer, many of his goals of six years earlier had been realized. The graduate office was firmly established in a strong and influential position, with adequate power to continue Ab's quest for quality at all levels of the University. "It was in his period as graduate dean," asserts Lewis Cochran, "that we really started developing a scholarly faculty, and he is the one, more than anybody else, who caused it to come about.... The good things we are seeing at the University now, by and large, are a consequence of those efforts then." Wimberly Royster, now graduate dean, perhaps adequately sums up most University opinion concerning Ab's accomplishments in the graduate office by saying simply, "I think he made a good graduate dean."

Kirwan won a position as Fulbright lecturer at the University of Vienna in 1966. Since Oswald had come to depend on him less and less for advice and consultation, Ab welcomed this opportunity to resign as graduate dean and take Betty to Austria for an unforgettably happy year.

Vienna's music and great charm had hardly dimmed in Ab's memory when Oswald announced his pending resignation in May 1968. He also announced, on June 24, that the two graceful new dormitory towers would be named in honor of Albert D. Kirwan and Sarah Blanding, a former dean of women at the University and president emeritus of Vassar College.[102] Meanwhile, Ab was elected to represent the faculty on an eight-member search committee to recommend a successor to the departing president.

Although Oswald's actions had split the faculty and generated political meddling from Frankfort, these expected problems became quite complicated by unexpected student-faculty confrontations involving the Vietnam war, university ideals and regulations, and educational processes in general. Dissatisfaction and anger were stirred to fury not only among students and university officials, but among parents and taxpayers and alumni. During the early summer of 1968, as the crisis deepened, Dr. Ralph Angelucci's search committee looked in vain for a man suitable for the increasingly tumultuous job of University president. A man was needed who could heal wounds. Gradually it occurred to the committee that they might have their man sitting among them—why not put Ab Kirwan in as acting president until time turned up exactly the man they wanted? Ab was willing. Angelucci thereupon got the Board of Trustees together for a caucus on this matter prior to their regular meeting. A. B. "Happy" Chandler here fought a final rearguard action for Vice President Glenwood Creech, casting the only vote against Ab. Kirwan became acting president at the regular Board meeting of July 19, 1968. At this meeting, Chandler did an aboutface, and "was the one who made the motion to elect Ab Kirwan as president of the University."[103] Ab knew what had happened, but he was always amused by the unabashed publicity seeking of his old friend Chandler. Happy thereafter gave Ab his undivided support, and Kirwan "always considered Chandler to be one of the better Board members."[104]

Kirwan's rich experience was once again available when needed, but his unenviable job was to clean up the battlefield while erecting a secure defense against any new outbreak. Until this was done, there would be "absolutely no possibility of getting a president to come to the University of Kentucky who might be outstanding.... Ab was almost essential to the transition from one president to another." Frank Dickey later wrote that "in his period as president, I feel that he brought the University back from the brink of real disaster." But at the time of Ab's acceptance a more emotional response is recalled by a colleague: "There was just a sigh of relief around here.... Everybody trusted him ... throughout the state and on the campus too. It would stabilize things."[105]

One of the keys Kirwan used to unlock the hostility of the Oswald era was Maxwell Place, the charming old presidential mansion. Indeed, Ab's first presidential act was to rescind the planned extension of the library to Rose Street, thereby destroying Maxwell Place. Before long, Betty had redecorated and refurnished the mansion in a way befitting its dignity. People from throughout the state joined students in attending various functions at the president's home. Enmities melted away in these friendly confines. Stuart Forth, former vice president for student affairs, confides that "the great style that Betty brought to her role ... must be the despair of half the presidential wives in the country.... Her efforts to make Maxwell Place again a major social center in Lexington as it had been in the days of previous presidents—notably McVey—I think were extraordinarily successful and effective."[106]

Kirwan's earliest major test as interim president came as a result of the 1968 election of Republican Louie B. Nunn as governor. Nunn would automatically become chairman of the Board of Trustees, yet "he was very anti-University of Kentucky." Shortly after his inauguration, Nunn presided over the December 1968 board meeting. It was normal procedure at the December meeting to set student room and board rates for the coming year, but Nunn did not know this. Harry Denham, a trustee at the time, recalls that the governor "was quite upset with the fact that we were raising room rates and board just at the time he was entering office." The governor said he had been warned that "at the first meeting they would try to raise everything.... He hadn't believed quite all of it, but now he was ready to believe it."

Ab immediately saw the danger of having an openly hostile governor in the midst of mounting student turmoil. Nunn was informed that there was absolutely no political bias involved and that the adjustment of student fees was always done in December. It took Ab time, but as Denham reports, "I think the governor finally became convinced, and over a period of a year or two he became a friend of the University. This was quite a surprise to many in Lexington."[107]

The student turmoil of the 1960s worried Ab. He knew that similar activity had manifested itself often in history, but he was greatly "puzzled by modern society's acceptance of it." He was aware, however, that much of the student activity was an overdue attack on long-ignored social evils. His interest in each student as an individual once again gave him perspective. "His liking for people [let him] see the student as a human being, not just a faceless kind of problem." On the other hand, Carl Cone reveals that he and Ab "used to joke quite a lot about our kids being 'squares,' and we were glad they were."[108]

As it was, President Kirwan was only put to one major test involving student activists, that on April 25, 1969. Vice President Forth had suspended three students who were charged with selling hard drugs by the city police on April 13. Betty Kirwan remembers that "for about a week nothing happened," but there were undercurrents of tension; then some of the professors became involved, and the situation began to grow more serious. Soon there was a march through the Administration Building, and signs appeared on campus fences: "Liberate Mrs. Kirwan." Meanwhile, on April 24, a Founders' Day celebration was held at Maxwell Place for Omicron Delta Kappa, the campus leadership organization founded by Ab and Emmett Milward in 1925. Betty now became the first president's wife to be elected "Sweetheart of ODK." The happy occasion was interrupted, however, by a gathering of some 300 students in the yard demanding that the president speak to them on the suspension issue. Ab refused, for "he had already made up his mind he would never address a mob of students."[109]

The next morning Ab met with his vice presidents and asked their opinions regarding the student demands. With the exception of Stuart Forth, each one thought that the indicted students should be readmitted. Ab then declared himself opposed to readmission. By this time about 1,000 youths had assembled outside the Administration Building. Their leader now came in and told Kirwan he would have to talk to them, for they were almost out of hand. Ab bluntly told the young man, "I don't have to speak to them because I didn't rouse them up—you did that. They are your responsibility, old boy, so you had better be sure you control them. If you get out there and lose control of them, then I'll handle them and you too."[110] With this, the startled leader stepped out and told the mob that Kirwan would not speak to them. They milled around briefly, then dispersed peacefully. The show was over.

News reports of Ab's firm stand brought favorable letters from everywhere. Typically, one from Louisville bearing twenty-eight signatures carried the writer's statement that given time, "I feel sure I could get 500 signatures of friends and acquaintances in support of your stand."[111] No letter carried a clearer assessment of what was at stake than that of Bruce Denbo:

> As one who was kicked out of school in the Huey Long censorship of the student newspaper at LSU more than 30 years ago, I can still remember what mistakes a university administration can make in handling a large group of ebullient and essentially irresponsible (but very idealistic) students. At this time, the Dean of Administration told a group of us in his office (when we said that this was a matter of principle) that, "Boys, when you get to be my age, you'll find that principle doesn't mean so much."
>
> It still does, whether 18 or 80, and I consider . . . that you have conducted yourself as a gentleman, a liberal, a scholar, and a Kentuckian. This is more important than it seems, because I believe that . . . the American people are perfectly capable . . . of withdrawing support from our institutions of education. . . . The crisis is graver than the irresponsibles imagine.[112]

Ab's presidency was not above honest criticism. Some thought "he should have acted more decisively" against the students. Others believed he too often looked for a "simple answer" to complex problems. Still others said that "he was not able to turn things over to people. He liked to be involved in many things which he just absolutely couldn't as president." Then, too, Ab caught some unthinking criticism "because he postponed a good many things for the incoming president, something he had to do, but which many people did not understand." His high position sometimes insulated him from certain needs. Wimberly Royster recalls "a dean of a college at that time who was saying we need some important decisions made right now, and you know Ab is out entertaining somebody, or Ab doesn't realize this is going on. It's not that he wouldn't do something about it, but he just doesn't realize it's going on." In spite of all, Ab pacified "town and gown," staving off possible disaster. Perhaps a majority of Kentuckians would have agreed with a Ravenna letterwriter who said "it is my hope that Kentucky educators are given consideration when choosing our permanent president. That last leap to California was nearly fatal."[113]

Opportunities to hire a permanent president increased as Ab's steady hand calmed the University community. By late 1968 the Board of Trustees believed it had its man in Otis Singletary, an author, historian, and executive vice chancellor for academic affairs at the University of Texas. Singletary accepted, and on May 27, 1969, Acting President Kirwan led him before the Board of Trustees for a final vote.

Otis Singletary was elected president of the University of Kentucky, but a surprise awaited Ab Kirwan. His old friend Happy Chandler took the floor, proposing that instead of acting president, "we let the records show that Albert Dennis Kirwan was the president of the University of Kentucky from the day that we selected him until his successor should have been elected and fully qualified." Chandler believed that no discussion was necessary, for "here is a man who has given his whole life to this institution and surely he must love it as perhaps no other person could. So let's stand." Everyone came to their feet, and Ab was unanimously installed as the seventh president of the University of Kentucky. He graciously acknowledged the honor: "This University has nourished me for most of my life; the kind remarks that Governor Chandler has just made about me have rendered me all but speechless. I thank you all from the bottom of my heart for this most recent testimony of your respect and your affection. . . . Thank you all so very much."[114]

Ab's presidency was hailed in a *Courier-Journal* editorial as one in which the "University has operated smoothly, calmly and with no sign of administrative lapse." The editor believed that Kirwan's "intellect and basic goodness seem always to show themselves to best advantage in times of crisis. . . . He has been chosen for difficult assignments repeatedly because people know that he is as dependable as he is versatile. He is a good man in whom people have faith."[115] As Betty Kirwan once said of her husband: "I guess next to me and his two sons he loved the University most. Many people have written and told me, 'He gave his life to the University.' And he truly did."[116]

Ab returned to teaching and writing after laying down the administrative gavel. He was not to find serenity, however, for the history department had changed as rapidly as the University and the world around it. The strong leadership of Thomas D. Clark was missing, and perhaps the respect for authority which had made possible that leadership. Many new professors had been hired to balance the rapid increase in student population. An extremely vicious dispute arose over the timing and prerogatives involved in a professorial appointment.[117] It was typical of most college level disputes—physically nonviolent, therefore loud and lengthy and damaging on a subtler, psychological level. Kirwan, in spite of his experience in past affairs, was unable to extricate himself from this one, and found it increasingly difficult to maintain his accustomed middle position in a divided department. Emotional wounds were inflicted, and these he took to his grave.[118]

Another emotionally scarring event took place during Ab's remaining months—the wanton vandalism of his serene old home in early November 1971. He and Betty returned from a trip out of town to find slashed furnishings, crushed silverware, and odds and ends broken and scattered everywhere. Ab had few if any enemies, and certainly none capable of such an attack. This, added to the fact that his large wall portrait was not touched, led most observers to conclude that the vandals had confused Ab's home with the nearly identical home of a local politician living a few doors down the street. Indeed, at the time of the crime the politician was involved in a heated local campaign. When one's home is vandalized, however, interpretations of the causes do little to assuage the frustration and anger produced by the effects.

All in all, Ab and Betty shared a most enjoyable day on November 29, 1971. They visited about town, returned home, and retired at midnight. But early the next morning Ab was awakened by breathing difficulties and an ambulance was dispatched for him. He died en route to the hospital. The trail Martin and Margaret had opened for him so long ago back in The Point had finally ended eighty miles away and three weeks short of his sixty-seventh birthday. His bluegrass-covered grave in Lexington's lovely cemetery is alongside many old University friends and colleagues. A heroic statue of Henry Clay surveys the entire scene from atop its lofty shaft. But Ab's is a simple marble marker, and the words inscribed upon it fairly embrace his well-lived life—"... truly, a man for all seasons."

Ab Kirwan at three, with brother Will (five) and sister Katherine (two). Below, Ab as captain of Louisville Male High School football team (1921).

Coach at the University of Kentucky *(Courier-Journal and Louisville Times).*

Below, the coaching staff in 1931: Kirwan with assistants Lloyd Ramsey, Frank Moseley, Bernie Shively, Gene Myers, Joe Rupert.

As head coach at duPont Manual High School, Louisville, 1935.

With Captain Joe Shepherd and players, 1939.

Frank Moseley, Bernie Shively, Ab Kirwan, 1931.

Dean Kirwan and Betty Kirwan chaperone a dance, 1952.

Betty Kirwan as editor of Kentucky Clubwoman Magazine, 1941 (Courier-Journal and Louisville Times).

After Kentucky's Sugar Bowl victory over Oklahoma, New Year's Day, 1951: President H. L. Donovan, Mrs. A. B. (Happy) Chandler, B. A. Shively, Governor Chandler, Betty and Ab Kirwan, Charles Grenrood.

Roger Mastin, Denny and Brit Kirwan at practice with the Wildcats, 1940 (Mack Hughes). Below, at the twenty-fifth reunion of the class of 1926: Eleanor Smith, Emmett Milward, Clifford Thompson, Frances Lee McLean, Ab Kirwan (Lexington Herald-Leader).

As chairman of the NCAA infractions committee, with Art Bergstrom, investigator (Lexington Herald-Leader).

Below, with President Thomas A. Spragens of Centre College (at left) and Vice President William R. Willard of U. K. Medical Center (Lexington Herald-Leader).

Presenting letters of appreciation to departing President John Oswald.

Presenting Optimist Cup to President Herman Donovan (Lexington Herald-Leader).

*With President Otis Singletary
(University of Kentucky Archives).*

With Marian Green, daughter of "Johnny Green of the Orphan Brigade" (Courier-Journal and Louisville Times).

Below, presenting University of Kentucky Fellowship to Thomas D. Clark, 1968.

At first meeting of the Editorial Board of the University Press of Kentucky: (clockwise) Dean William M. Jones, Berea College; Dr. Victor B. Howard, Morehead State University; Dr. Lowell H. Harrison, Western Kentucky University; Dr. Richard M. Kain, University of Louisville; Dr. Albert D. Kirwan, University of Kentucky; Dean Frederic D. Ogden, Eastern Kentucky University; Dr. Charles T. Hazelrigg, Centre College; Vance Ramage, Murray State University; Dr. Henry E. Cheaney, Kentucky State University (Courier-Journal and Louisville Times).

With Vassar President Sarah Blanding at the dedication of Blanding and Kirwan Towers (Lexington Herald-Leader).

Ab and Betty Kirwan welcome new faculty members. Below, hospitality at Maxwell Place.

Ab and Betty Kirwan after his installation as seventh president of the University of Kentucky; below, the president at Homecoming (both Lexington Herald-Leader).

On Commencement Day (Lexington Herald-Leader).

NOTES

[1] The material concerning Albert Kirwan's ancestry and childhood is compiled from a letter from his sister Susan (Mrs. C. J. McDevitt), dated November 15, 1972; from an interview with his brother, William English, on June 1, 1972, and from conversations with Mrs. Albert D. Kirwan. A surprising amount of supplemental material is found under the Kirwan name in the appropriate year of *Caron's Louisville Directory*, which includes the family's occupations, house numbers, the Louisville environment, and advertisements for the family lumberyard.

[2] Louisville's streets were renumbered in 1908-1909. The old numbers were 1718 Mellwood and 1226 Fulton.

[3] Albert D. Kirwan, "Some Memories of My Life," electronically taped in 1971 and transcribed by the author. Unless otherwise indicated, subsequent direct quotations by Kirwan are taken from this source. Tapes in possession of Mrs. Albert D. Kirwan.

[4] Louisville *Courier-Journal*, November 26, 27, 1920.

[5] Ibid., November 25, 1921.

[6] Harry lived at 142 North Hite and Joseph Ross at 105.

[7] Kirwan in 1971 recorded that "I never even got a letter from the coach or from the athletic director, although I did get invitations from other universities to the north and to the east."

[8] Lexington *Herald*, October 1, 1922.

[9] Interview with Albert Tanner, Maxwell Place, May 11, 1972; Lexington *Herald*, October 21, November 12, 1922.

[10] Lexington *Herald*, November 4, 1923.

[11] Ibid., December 1, 1923.

[12] Ibid., November 2, 1924.

[13] Ibid., November 1, 1925.

[14] Ibid., November 27, 1925.

[15] Ibid., November 25, 1926.

[16] Louisville *Courier-Journal*, November 25, 1927; November 30, 1928; November 28, 29, 1929; November 28, 1930; November 27, 1931.

[17] Mrs. Albert D. Kirwan to author, September 12, 1972.

[18] A newspaper clipping of Ripley's use of this record is in the possession of Mrs. Albert D. Kirwan.

[19] Interview with Mrs. Albert D. Kirwan, October 26, 1972.

[20] Ibid.; Joe Creason to author, March 7, 1974; Barbara L. Pickett, Louisville Free Public Library, to author, March 28, 1974.

[21] Interview with William McCubbin, August 25, 1972. McCubbin also played and coached for Kirwan at UK in the 1930s and 1940s. Presently, he is athletics director at VPI.

[22] Louisville *Courier-Journal*, November 25, 1932; December 1, 1933.

[23] Interview with William McCubbin, August 25, 1972; Louisville *Courier-Journal*, October 14, 1934.

[24] Interview with William McCubbin, August 25, 1972; Louisville *Courier-Journal*, October 21, 1934; interview with Mrs. Albert D. Kirwan, December 6, 1972.

[25] Louisville *Courier-Journal*, November 30, 1934.

[26] Years later Ab was to recall this friendly rivalry in a different context. It was 1952, and as Kentucky's Dean Kirwan he stood before the executive committee of the Southeastern Conference to appeal its decision to suspend

the Wildcat basketball team over a gambling scandal. See Albert D. Kirwan, "Statement before Executive Committee of Southeastern Conference," pp. 102-12. Typed document in possession of Mrs. Albert D. Kirwan, pp. 1-2. (Hereafter, page references are to the typed document, "Kirwan's SEC Statement.")

[27] Interview with Harry Denham, October 26, 1972; interview with Mrs. Albert D. Kirwan, October 26, 1972. Charles G. Talbert, *The University of Kentucky: The Maturing Years* (Lexington, 1965), pp. 129-30. Interestingly, Denham played for Kirwan at UK, and later he and teammate William Black were members of the Board of Trustees that voted Kirwan into the presidency.

[28] *The Kentuckian*, 1939, p. 102.

[29] "Kirwan's SEC Statement," p. 2; "Court of General Sessions of the County of New York. In the Matter of the Basketball Investigation. Before: Hon. Saul S. Streit, Judge of the Court of General Session. New York, February 27, 1952," pp. 22, 26, typed document in UK Athletics Department files. (Hereafter, "Kirwan to Streit.")

[30] "Kirwan to Streit," p. 11.

[31] *The Kentuckian*, 1940, pp. 117-20.

[32] Ibid., 1941, pp. 188-94; interview with Mrs. Albert D. Kirwan, August 25, 1972.

[33] *The Kentuckian*, 1944, p. 115.

[34] Papers of Herman Lee Donovan, University of Kentucky Archives, file 6, drawer 3, ASTP folder. (Hereafter, Donovan Papers.) See also, Herman Lee Donovan, *Keeping the University Free and Growing* (Lexington, 1959), pp. 56-59.

[35] Interview with Thomas D. Clark, October 13, 1972. Unless otherwise indicated, subsequent direct quotations by Clark are taken from this interview.

[36] Mrs. Albert D. Kirwan to author, September 12, 1972; Registrars' Reports from UK and UL on A. D. Kirwan's academic record to author, February 8 and 13, 1974, respectively.

[37] *The Kentuckian*, 1945, pp. 84-91.

[38] Interview with Mrs. Albert D. Kirwan, October 26, 1972; see also, Donovan, *Keeping the University Free and Growing*, p. 87.

[39] Ibid.

[40] Interview with Brit Kirwan, June 1, 1972.

[41] Interview with Mrs. Albert D. Kirwan, October 26, 1972; Louisville *Courier-Journal*, February 6, 1951.

[42] Interview with Thomas D. Clark, October 13, 1972; Donovan, *Keeping the University Free and Growing*, pp. vii, 20-27.

[43] Donovan Papers, file 4, drawer 4, contain hundreds of interesting letters concerning Kirwan's day-by-day job as dean of men. Donovan himself wrote later that the veterans "accepted the leadership of the dean of men, and helped him in establishing a high standard of citizenship [on campus and off], a standard that has seldom been equaled in this country." Donovan, *Keeping the University Free and Growing*, p. 88.

[44] Typed transcript of "Conversation with Dr. Singletary," recorded September 8, 1969, UKTV center. Manuscript in possession of Mrs. Albert D. Kirwan.

[45] Interview with Mrs. Albert D. Kirwan, March 17, 1973.

[46] Donovan, *Keeping the University Free and Growing*, p. 89; interview with Carl Cone, May 10, 1972.

[47] Donovan Papers, file 4, drawer 4, letter dated June 22, 1948.

[48] Donovan, *Keeping the University Free and Growing*, pp. 104, 116.

[49] "Kirwan to Streit," p. 17.
[50] "Answers to an Inquiry. From the NCAA Sub-Committee on Infractions: to the President of the University of Kentucky," p. 6, typed document in UK Athletics Department files.
[51] New York *Times,* January 14, 15, 1950.
[52] Nashville *Banner,* January 13, 1951. Ab's speech also received notice in the New York *Times,* January 13, 1951.
[53] Lexington *Herald,* January 14, 1951.
[54] "Kirwan to Streit," p. 28.
[55] "Minutes of the Meeting of the Board of Directors of the University of Kentucky Athletic Association on Sunday, March 2, 1952," p. 22, typed copy in possession of Mrs. Albert D. Kirwan.
[56] Ibid., pp. 3, 4, 7.
[57] Ibid., p. 20; Lexington *Herald,* March 3, 1952.
[58] "Kirwan to Streit," pp. 37-38.
[59] Frankfort *State-Journal,* November 27, 1940; "Kirwan's SEC Statement," p. 8.
[60] Louisville *Courier-Journal,* August 3, 1952; "Kirwan to Streit," p. 28.
[61] "Kirwan to Streit," pp. 43, 45.
[62] Ibid., pp. 52-53.
[63] Interview with Mrs. Albert D. Kirwan, May 6, 1973.
[64] Lexington *Herald,* November 4, 1952; interview with Mrs. Albert D. Kirwan, October 26, 1972.
[65] "Kirwan's SEC Statement," p. 6; interview with Mrs. Albert D. Kirwan, October 26, 1972.
[66] A. D. Kirwan to Frank N. Gardner, Des Moines, September 26, 1952; interview with Mrs. Albert D. Kirwan, October 26, 1972.
[67] Don Flatt to Mrs. Albert D. Kirwan, January 13, 1972; Bill Cooper to Mrs. Albert D. Kirwan, December 2, 1972; interview with Ray Bennett, June 2, 1972.
[68] Interview with James Hopkins, June 2, 1972.
[69] A. D. Kirwan to A. D. Albright, November 18, 1970.
[70] *The Kentucky Kernel,* December 1, 1971.
[71] Mimeographed form with typed comment entitled "Annual Evaluation of Faculty Achievement," dated March 7, 1968. In possession of Mrs. Albert D. Kirwan.
[72] Interview with Harry Denham, October 26, 1972.
[73] Interview with Earl Wallace, May 12, 1972. Not a hint of contradiction emerged to contest this impression held by the many persons I interviewed in preparing this book; Betty Kirwan was seen typically as "his greatest strength," "the good woman behind him," "his best asset." Interview with Ray Bennett, June 2, 1972.
[74] Charles Dollar to Mrs. Albert D. Kirwan, December 14, 1971.
[75] Interview with Denny Kirwan, November 27, 1972.
[76] Ibid.; interview with Mrs. Albert D. Kirwan, October 26, 1972.
[77] Interviews with Wimberly Royster, Mrs. Albert D. Kirwan, and Earl Wallace, on May 11, 5, and 12, 1972, respectively; Louisville *Courier-Journal,* June 3, 1969.
[78] Interview with Denny Kirwan, as told by Ab's grandson, Patrick Lynn Kirwan, November 27, 1972.
[79] Interview with Mrs. Albert D. Kirwan, September 12, 1972; Rupert Vance, *Journal of Southern History,* 17 (August 1951): 412; C. Vann Woodward, *American Historical Review,* 56 (July 1951): 918; A. D. Kirwan to Dr.

James W. Silver, July 2, 1963. The usual sources fail to reveal the periodical carrying Simkins's review, although a typed copy is in the possession of Mrs. Albert D. Kirwan; A. H. George, Greenwood, Miss., to Bell I. Wiley, Memphis, Tenn., February 22, 1951, letter in possession of Mrs. Albert D. Kirwan.

[80] Herbert Weaver, *Journal of Southern History*, 22 (August 1956): 394.

[81] New York *Herald-Tribune*, April 17, 1960.

[82] A. D. Kirwan to Thomas D. Clark, July 14, 1962; Albert D. Kirwan, *John J. Crittenden: The Struggle for the Union* (Lexington, 1962), p. 412; Roy F. Nichols, *American Historical Review*, 68 (July 1963): 1085; Robert G. Gunderson, *Journal of Southern History*, 29 (May 1963): 265.

[83] Bennett H. Wall, "Annual Report," *Journal of Southern History*, 21 (May 1965): 172; interview with Mrs. Albert D. Kirwan, October 26, 1972.

[84] Carl N. Degler, *American Historical Review*, 72 (July 1967): 1501; Rice Estes, *Library Journal*, 92 (March 15, 1967): 1154; *The Choice*, 4 (June 1967): 470; Joseph Steelman, *Journal of Southern History*, 33 (August 1967): 377-79.

[85] Thomas P. Govan, *Journal of American History*, 56 (June 1969): 136.

[86] Interview with James Hopkins, June 2, 1972; James Hopkins to author, May 28, 1973.

[87] Louisville *Courier-Journal*, October 5, 1969.

[88] Interview with Thomas D. Clark, October 13, 1972; interview with Bruce Denbo, December 20, 1972.

[89] Ab's friend Stuart Forth backs Clark's assertion, revealing that Kirwan, when pressed beyond his usual disclaimers regarding administrative work, admitted that he liked it immensely. Interview with Stuart Forth, May 10, 1972.

[90] Thomas D. Clark insists: "That appointment was made, like so many key appointments at the University of Kentucky, with no one knowing what was going on."

[91] Interview with Wimberly Royster, May 11, 1972.

[92] Ibid.

[93] Interview with Lewis Cochran, February 8, 1974. Unless otherwise indicated, subsequent direct quotations by Cochran are taken from this interview.

[94] Louisville *Courier-Journal*, January 22, 1963; Lexington *Leader*, January 21, 1963.

[95] Interview with Mrs. Albert D. Kirwan, October 26, 1972; interview with Carl Cone, May 10, 1972; Talbert, *The University of Kentucky*, p. 197.

[96] Interview with Lewis Cochran, February 8, 1974. A puzzling rotation policy relieved fit and unfit alike from various departmental chairmanships. Thomas D. Clark, for example, was rotated, although his history department was one of only two departments on campus to have achieved national ranking at that time.

[97] Interview with Mrs. Albert D. Kirwan, March 17, 1973.

[98] Nevertheless, Ab's friend Earl Wallace insists that "I always thought he had a rather throttling influence on Oswald to the extent he could, but nobody could throttle Oswald. That is, I think, a general consensus." Interview with Earl Wallace, May 12, 1972. Mrs. Albert D. Kirwan offers some support for Wallace's view by revealing that Ab advised Oswald against removing Dean of Education Lyman Ginger, a man of great political power throughout the state: "Don't fire Ginger, for it will pull the wrath of the state's teachers down on you. The Education College isn't worth it to you anyway." Oswald paid no attention and removed Ginger, generating the

political whirlwind that soon swept through his office. Interview with Mrs. Albert D. Kirwan, March 17, 1973.

[99] Interview with Lewis Cochran, February 8, 1974.

[100] Ibid.; interview with Mrs. Albert D. Kirwan, October 23, 1973.

[101] Interview with Donald Leigh, May 12, 1973.

[102] John W. Oswald to "Dear Ab," June 26, 1968. Ab responded to Oswald's announcement: "It is an honor few men could merit and one which certainly I do not. But the fact that you think I do means much indeed to me. Thanks! Thanks! Thanks!" A. D. Kirwan to "Dear Jack," July 3, 1968.

[103] Interview with Harry Denham, October 26, 1972.

[104] Interview with Mrs. Albert D. Kirwan, October 26, 1972.

[105] Interview with Harry Denham, October 26, 1972; Frank Dickey to Mrs. Albert D. Kirwan, December 1, 1971; interview with Carl Cone, May 10, 1972.

[106] Interview with Mrs. Albert D. Kirwan, October 26, 1972; interview with Stuart Forth, May 10, 1972.

[107] Interview with Harry Denham, October 26, 1972.

[108] Interview with Stuart Forth, May 10, 1972; interview with Carl Cone, May 10, 1972.

[109] Lexington *Herald,* April 14, 24, 25, 1969; interview with Mrs. Albert D. Kirwan, March 17, 1973.

[110] Ab had access to the national guard and the city police and was determined to use them if need be. Governor Nunn later told Betty Kirwan that he had called the Board of Trustees together after the student march through the Administration Building. He said he "would have acted if any threat arose against Dr. Kirwan." Interview with Mrs. Albert D. Kirwan, March 17, 1973. See also, Louisville *Times,* April 25, 1969 (evening edition), for photos and details of the affair at the Administration Building.

[111] James L. Calvert, Louisville, to "Ab Kirwan, Acting Pres.," April 30, 1969.

[112] Bruce F. Denbo to "Dear Ab," April 25, 1969.

[113] Interview with Donald Leigh, May 12, 1972; interview with Stuart Forth, May 10, 1972; interview with Wimberly Royster, May 11, 1972; interview with Harry Lancaster, May 10, 1972; A. F. Bush, Ravenna, Ky., to Editor, Lexington *Herald,* April 29, 1969 (typed carbon copy in possession of Mrs. Albert D. Kirwan).

[114] Typed copy of "Chandler's Tribute to Dr. Kirwan 5/27/69," in possession of Mrs. Albert D. Kirwan. See also, Lexington *Leader,* May 29, 1969.

[115] Louisville *Courier-Journal,* June 3, 1969.

[116] Mrs. Albert D. Kirwan to author, September 12, 1972.

[117] Interview with Thomas D. Clark, October 13, 1972. Many others were interviewed concerning this, and some refused an interview.

[118] Interview with Mrs. Albert D. Kirwan, March 17, 1973.

II.
Writings & Speeches

INTRODUCTION

Albert D. Kirwan's influence reached far beyond his classroom, for he touched the hearts and minds of the thousands who read his books and articles on Mississippi politics, the Confederate homefront, the statesman John J. Crittenden, the soldier Johnny Green, and the South since the Civil War. In addition to the use of the printed word, Kirwan spread his ideas almost continually over a thirty-five year period through addresses before historical associations, banquets, high school and college commencement gatherings, athletics assemblies, and radio and television audiences.

As author or speaker Kirwan seldom strayed far from the subjects that most interested him—history, the South, education, athletics, politics, the Civil War, and civil rights. Although seemingly unrelated, Ab's liberal spirit dictated his approach to each of these topics and reflected a pattern of thought unifying them all. This unity was the result of Kirwan's unswerving adherence to a basic principle of Christianity—the essential sameness of all people—and this principle formed the core of his liberalism.

Kirwan was no armchair liberal, but a combination of action and thought—the old philosopher king. He was responsive and responsible, acting upon his liberal beliefs; in no way did he resemble the alienated intellectual. Indeed, the thinker is ever in danger of his own logic leading him finally into impossible situations. Kirwan early recognized through his active involvement in the affairs of this world that one can reach a point beyond which logic no longer holds. The liberal jurist Oliver Wendell Holmes defended freedom of speech to the limits of logic, and would go no further; for no person has the freedom to shout "Fire!" in a crowded theater, he said, if there is in fact no fire. Kirwan would have agreed with Holmes, believing as he did that the rights of one man end where those of others begin. His courageous refusal to reinstate the three students indicted for selling narcotics in spite of majority pressures is a direct reflection of this belief. While students did not have the right to engage in criminal activity, they certainly did have the right to expect his protection against such activities. For him, then, liberalism never became confused with license. In fact, given his independence of mind, it is hard to say whether his outlook was actually Kirwan liberalism or liberal Kirwanism!

The first part of this selection of speeches and letters indicates the wide range of Kirwan's thoughts on education. He believed that a good education has always been difficult to obtain and is a continual process for the learner. The writings included here reveal Kirwan in many different moods, but whether he was discussing "effete intellectuals," plotting the future course of his university, or speaking out on the shady side of college sports, his opinions were always frank and sincerely expressed. Here too we catch a glimpse of the man who could be eloquently tongue-in-cheek, mingling warm praise and gentle humor to comment on the foibles and accomplishments of several of his fellow educators.

The second section focuses on Kirwan's concern with the Civil War; here he writes with great authority on the South's dependence on "King Cotton," and the shift of Kentucky sentiment as the battles opened. Moreover, he completely shatters a Lincoln myth by revealing Old Abe's naiveté as civil conflict neared. Whatever Lincoln became later, at the time of his 1860 election "and for some months thereafter, he was a plain country lawyer with narrowly limited background." He became just as stubborn as his Republican advisors, rejecting Crittenden's plan of compromise and with it the last real chance to avoid Civil War. In short, there is relevance aplenty for today's world in the frustrating experiences of Crittenden in 1860-1861.

The third section reveals Kirwan's great concern with civil rights, whether tested in peace or by war. He wrote extensively about the causes of southern violence, the inroads made during the Civil War on personal rights, and the long-ignored grievances of the American black.

Kirwan's legal training sharpened his understanding of politics, the theme of the final section. He adds much to our comprehension of the complicated Kentucky court struggle of the 1820s, clarifying the complexities of the affair considerably through the simple power of his prose. Kirwan saw this decade as a halfway house on the road to populism, for the economic class conflict that emerged during this time was to serve as a "harbinger of national issues." Crittenden learned this lesson, but Clay did not, and Kirwan believed that Clay here may have lost an ingredient essential to his future political success. In any event, one can only wonder how Kirwan's interpretation of Clay would have changed if Providence had granted him time to complete "Old Harry's" biography. Finally, this section includes

Kirwan's dispassionate analysis of the programs put forth by Theodore H. Bilbo and James K. Vardaman, an excellent illustration of the ideological independence with which he thought and wrote.

Here indeed was a liberal and entirely humane scholar who knew how to think for himself!

EDUCATION

What Can My Son Do with History   81

Not a Map, but a Compass   82

History and the True Intellectual   84

The Modern Campus Must Learn Self-Government   85

Future Plans for the University of Kentucky   90

Not a Man of Boundless Patience   94

You Made Us What We Are Today   98

Statement before Executive Committee of Southeastern Conference   102

WHAT CAN MY SON DO WITH HISTORY

Now, commencement speakers have from time immemorial, been addicted to philosophizing and giving advice to their young listeners, knowing all the time that they will little note nor long remember what is said. But it is a worthy tradition, and one that I do not wish to depart from. So, I will make my message as brief and clearcut as I can.

In the first place I would urge you to read books. You have been introduced to some great literature in your high school years. Build on this. Life is too short and the universe is too large for one to learn by personal experience. Books are a short-cut to the wisdom of the ages. What great men have thought and done, their successes and failures are contained within library shelves. Do not neglect these riches of the ages, which are yours for the asking.

In the second place I would urge you to learn for the love of learning. Sometimes people of a practical turn of mind foolishly turn their children from theoretical studies which they love to technical or professional studies which they do not love, because there is "more money in it." Now, business is important and businessmen are important people without whom our society could not function. But scholars and scientists are important people, too. And while a certain amount of money—enough to meet modest daily needs—is important to us all, the great scientific discoveries and the great artistic masterpieces have not been created by people whose primary concern was making money.

My own discipline is history, and I am sometimes told by a disturbed parent that his son wants to study history, but they think he should study engineering or pharmacy because "there's more money in it." "What," he asks, "can my son do with history?"

I generally reply that Shakespeare did a good deal with history, and that in more recent times Winston Churchill, Douglas Southall Freeman and others have done a good deal with it too. Even Theodore Roosevelt and Woodrow Wilson wrote history as well as made it, and Franklin Roosevelt and Harry Truman, in their presidential careers drew continually on their knowledge of history.

But, my young friends, there are things in this world which are important, but which do not have a dollar sign on them. One does not join a church, I hope, because it will help him in business. A man does not marry a wife so that she may support him. A father does not calculate, when he spends money on his children's welfare, what return in dollars he will get out of it. No, the truly important things in your lives, you will find, can neither be bought nor sold. True happiness, I'm sure you will find, will only come as the result of a life spent in interesting, congenial, and useful work.

*(from Commencement Address,
Lafayette High School, Lexington, 1960)*

NOT A MAP, BUT A COMPASS

I am very pleased to be with you here this morning. You know, this is familiar ground to me. I was born and grew up in Louisville, and as a boy I roamed the fields between here and St. Matthews. And as a member of the football team at Male High School I played on your athletics field here against your predecessors in this corps.

My own delight at being here is balanced with an understanding, based on memory of several decades ago, that a speaker on such an occasion should seek clarity and brevity. You want to get on to the congratulations, to the gatherings, to the final formation after these ceremonies. I have not forgotten, but for a few moments let us honor this milestone in your lives by some thoughtful and reflective comments.

For graduation is a milestone. It recognizes that each of you has completed satisfactorily a course of study, and now the members of this class are eligible for a diploma of graduation. But the completion of one task means that we are ready to start another. Therefore, on this occasion we look not only behind us with a sense of having accomplished something but also to the future—to the commencement of another major undertaking in your lives.

If I should let my remarks here this morning be given a theme or a title, I think I would choose the words "Not a Map, but a Compass."

If you were starting out on a journey, as indeed you are, it would be helpful if you could have a map, indicating the point from which you start, the route you would follow to reach your desired destination, detours to avoid, speed limits, accommodations. A map would be helpful for geographical travel, but it would not suffice for the journey you are about to undertake. The map that I followed would not do for you. For times and conditions change, and you may wish and need to go places that I will not have experienced.

And so I could not possibly give you a map for the next half-century of your lives. In the first place, you would not want it. It would limit and stultify you. There is a desire in each of us for freedom, for adventure into the unknown. This has been a driving force of the human race from the beginning of history and probably before. An ambition to scale the heights in order to see what is beyond.

In the second place, I couldn't devise such a map for you even if you wanted one. Neither I nor your teachers nor your parents can foretell with any precision the terrain you are going to travel in your life. If we should caution you with anecdotes which begin, "When I was your age . . .," or tell you, "I remember when . . .," we run the risk of wasting your time with irrelevance and with idealized misrepresentation.

We cannot give you a map because we cannot foretell the future. We can only say with certainty—there will be change and new directions for each of you. Most of you will have several different vocations. Time was when a young man might say, "I'm going to be a lawyer," or "a doctor," or "a soldier," or "a teacher," and that would be it. Today he might start out as a lawyer, then perhaps join a corporation, move on to a government job, and perhaps eventually become a teacher. Statistics suggest that on the average each of you will change vocational directions as many as five times in your life span.

Not only will your occupation be modified, but you yourself will change. Medical science in your lifetime may give you a new heart, a new liver or kidney, tie in a plastic artery. We could go on listing the changes in your life as we think together of what lies ahead . . . of the new career you are about to begin. Your unmapped future may well contain space travel. It will contain happiness, sorrow, tragedy, reward, perhaps personal injustice. But wherever you go and whatever careers you follow, there exist certain characteristics, certain qualities of heart and mind that will determine how satisfying your life will be to you.

When I was in high school I had a teacher who urged us lads to seek higher education because of the worldly rewards it would bring. He had a chart which he used to use to demonstrate that with each additional year of schooling one's earning ability (on the average) would show a marked increase. I have no doubt his chart was correct statistically, but as a teacher he was a complete failure. For he was giving us shallow and feeble principles to guide us through our lives.

*(from Commencement Address,
Kentucky Military Institute, 1969)*

HISTORY AND THE TRUE INTELLECTUAL

As for the "worth" attendant upon the study of history, it seems to me that the wisest of historians are in agreement that the past is no clue to the future. Henry Adams, grandson of President John Quincy Adams and himself a distinguished historian, attempted in the early years of this century to reduce history to some kind of a scientific formula which would accurately predict the future. But most of his contemporaries as well as present day historians I know think he failed completely.

But the study of history I find, while it cannot predict the future, will help explain how we arrived at the place we are in the present. I liken it to a map without roads. It shows where we began and where we are now, but it does not have a red-penciled route marked for the spot we desire to reach. But even though it does not give these explicit instructions, it does, nevertheless, give us a sense of direction so as to keep us from doubling back on our own path. And, if we are wise enough to profit some from the wisdom that was characteristic of some of them. But to discredit history as worthless would be like saying that loss of memory would not be harmful to an individual. For history is society's memory.

I agree with you that many so-called intellectuals would rather be clever and shocking than right. But these people, it seems to me, have nothing of real significance to say: and they satisfy their ego by what you call "nit-picking," and by writing in a jargon that most people do not understand. . . .

Many "intellectuals" are, I fear, the "effete snobs," Mr. Agnew called them. But these are phonys [sic]. The true intellectual, in my opinion, is one who tries to absorb and to advance the great intellectual achievements of the past in both the ancient and the modern world.

(in answer to a letter from Wayman Thomason, March 9, 1970)

THE MODERN CAMPUS MUST LEARN SELF-GOVERNMENT

I little thought when I was asked last summer to serve what all of us then believed would be a brief term as acting president of this university that I would be presiding at these graduation exercises in this month of May. But so it is. And I shall be ever grateful to Governor Nunn and the Board of Trustees for their confidence as well as for the generous, unstinted support they have given me throughout the year. I am grateful, too, to the administrative leaders who have given me wise advice and stout support, and to countless members of the faculty and student body who have been so thoughtful and kind during these months and who have made this a pleasant, exciting, and indeed a happy experience for me.

But, having served here under the last four presidents, all of whom I loved and admired; and having been a student here when the presence of President Patterson was still more than a memory, I am overawed at the thought of leaning on a podium that might have been designed for a McVey, a Donovan, a Dickey, or an Oswald. The occasion reminds me of an incident in the life of the celebrated 18th century Irish barrister, Sir John Curran. In a Galway trial he and opposing counsel engaged in a debate over the meaning of the words *also* and *likewise*. The trial judge, a newcomer, growing impatient of the semantics, ordered the lawyers to proceed with the trial because, he said, the words were synonymous.

"Your honor," said Sir John, "I beg to differ. To illustrate, let me point out that before you were appointed to this bench your predecessor, Sir Patrick Sarsfield, presided over this court with dignity and distinction. Now you preside over this court *also,* but not *likewise.*" What effect Sir John's comment had on the outcome of the trial the chronicler sayeth not.

I'm sure I have made many mistakes during the past year, but I have not agonized over making them. When decisions had to be made I sought advice from many sources, listened to all points of view, then acted on my own best judgment and never looked back. In this respect I am like an old baseball umpire I used to know. "I miss a lot of times," he said, "but I miss them quick."

For you, the members of the class of 1969, I shall always have a special affection. There are all sorts of superlatives I could use in describing you without in any way distorting the literal truth. I could say, for instance, that you are the handsomest and most charming class graduated during my administration. I could say also that you are the most learned, the most intelligent, the best educated—and it would all be true. But I shall not say these things. I shall say, instead, that you are what you are: decent, responsible, industrious, earnest, attractive young men and women, whose progress and whose careers I shall watch hereafter with more than ordinary pride and concern. And when you return for your 25th reunion, as I hope all of you will, I trust you will permit me to join you in celebrating that festive event.

It used to be customary on occasions such as this for the president or for some substitute whom he called in, to deliver a sermon-like address ending generally with an inspirational exhortation. But I shall spare you that today. In the first place, I am not a man of the cloth, and I have no skill at sermon composition or delivery. I have spent too much of my life digging into the past, trying to learn from whence we came, how we got where we are and whither we are headed. It has been a very interesting study even though I am not at all confident that I have found the answers I sought. In the second place, you are far too intelligent and too sophisticated to long remember any inspirational admonitions I might give you—even if I were so inclined, which I am not.

But you have now reached a stage in your careers when you must become responsible participants in the painful and sometimes agonizing decision-making process in the society that will soon be yours to manage. Your education has been largely directed toward giving you an understanding of that society in its diversities and complexities. If you run true to form, and I rather think you will exceed than disappoint our expectations, you are destined to have positions of leadership in that society—as parents, business and professional leaders, mayors, legislators, congressmen, governors, judges, teachers, perhaps a cabinet member of two, maybe even a President of the United States. And so, if I may, I shall take just a few minutes to talk about some of the difficulties that now beset our society the solutions for which are not yet agreed on—problems of a formidable nature that you must grapple with if you are to pass on to your children a world no worse than you are inheriting.

A series of tragic events over the last two generations has shattered the self-complacency of the age I grew up in. Grandiose schemes for abolishing war, stamping out poverty, integrating the races have led to disillusion. Confidence in the future of the country and of the world order are no longer taken for granted. Affluence to an unprecedented degree for the many has not resulted in prosperity for those in poverty. On the one hand, men have organized themselves and their knowledge and resources with such skill, vision, and courage that it is almost certain we will soon put a man on the moon. On the other hand, we are unable to build the houses we need, move traffic through our choking cities, or keep ourselves from polluting the very air we breathe and the water we drink. We can train and organize the skilled manpower needed to launch and recover Apollo, but we have been unable to train the unskilled who stand hopeless in our ghetto streets. We have conquered polio, but we have not been able to prevent pellagra, rickets, and other diseases of malnutrition.

In our conquest of nature we have lost contact with natural things. In our concentration on electronics, on spacecraft and missiles, we have neglected things more fundamental. We can fly from coast to coast in three hours or less, but workers in our great cities must spend that much time each day getting to and from work. Our lakes and rivers, once so fresh and nourishing in a more primitive age, are now so fouled that someone said, "If you fall in, you do not drown, you dissolve."

Brief reflection on these questions suggests that our society has been somewhat misguided in the fixing of its priorities. Fortunately, many of these priorities are now under review. A new and penetrating look is being taken and new appraisals made of Vietnam, of sociological problems of the ghettos, of the ethics of power-politics as played by the two super-powers. Indeed, as to the real limits of the power of the super-states to control events even in their own particular spheres of influence, witness the restlessness in Czechoslovakia, Yugoslavia, and Roumania vis-à-vis Russia on the one hand; and our own inability to control events in Southeast Asia and in Latin America.

But I suggest that there is one mortal danger of even graver consequences facing the democratic nations of the world at this particular moment in our history. This is a problem that we have not yet actually come to grips with. It is the question of our ability to govern ourselves, particularly in the colleges and universities of this country, institutions which should be the very center of enlightenment and reason. Everywhere we look these days authority is being challenged: authority of parents, the church, the schools, the state, the universities. The chief danger in this challenge is the resort to physical force to achieve demands or else the intimidation of officials by the threat of force. To defy the militant demands on the universities or to put them down with force when they resort to force generally results in campus chaos. To appease them invites further assaults. Either course broadens the growing chasm between parents, alumni, and the larger community of citizens on the one hand and the university communities on the other. This could well lead, as one university president has warned, "to the suppression of the liberty and autonomy that are the life blood of a university." It may very well lead, he added, "to a rebirth of fascism unless we ourselves are ready to take a stand." Indeed, it well might lead to a revival of the notorious witch-hunt era of Senator Joe McCarthy.

At Cornell, as one pundit wrote, "guns met reason—and reason lost." Every university president is now in a three-way bind: campus lawlessness, defecting or nonsupporting faculties, and an outraged public. Unless students, faculties, and administrators find ways of renewing their mutual trust and confidence in one another, the universities will be the ultimate victims of these tragic events.

Reasons for administration surrender on many campuses are obvious: the risk of violence and consequent blood-shed is something no college wants or is ready to assume responsibility for. The alternative is a toughness alien to university tradition and to the academic mind. Meanwhile, time and public tolerance may be running out on the universities. Lawmakers everywhere are warning: "Take charge, or we'll do it."

Action in statehouses around the country from Massachusetts to California and from Wisconsin to Florida show clearly that university authorities are losing public confidence in their ability to keep order on their campuses. Surrender of faculties to intimidation by student and faculty militants raises the fundamental question of the competency of the university community to govern itself according to its own regulations carefully worked out with full student participation.

One of the most extreme laws is that recently passed in West Virginia. It provides that in efforts to suppress unlawful gatherings anyone who refuses to help the police when called on "shall be deemed a rioter." Police officials would be held guiltless if they killed anyone ... even a spectator. On the other hand, if any police officer or public official was injured or killed, "all persons engaged in such assemblage" would be deemed guilty under the law.

But the threat of reaction comes not only from statehouses, but also from our own campuses. A growing number of right-wing students have also lost confidence in university self-government and are preparing to take direct action. Student groups such as The Young Americans for Freedom and The National Youth Alliance are preparing to meet violence with violence. This mobilization of the campus right adds still another dimension to the threat to university self-government.

Fortunately for us here at Kentucky those students who would urge violence, if there be any, are so few in number, and the overwhelming majority of our students are so committed to reason and non-violence that thus far we are one of few major universities in the land that has suffered no outburst of violence. Indeed, save for the disagreement of a few weeks ago this school year has been one of undisturbed and halcyon calm. Ordinarily one does not expect a good-conduct medal for not violating the law, but in these troubled times I might well be charged with an obtuse lack of appreciation if I should not note on this occasion their remarkably good behavior and commend them for it.

And so, members of the class of 1969, for all but those relatively few of you who will continue here in graduate or professional programs, this day will mark your physical separation from this campus. Within a decade or two at the most you will be taking your places as natural leaders in communities wherever you may be. But you will not be severed in spirit from this place. You now belong to a large and evergrowing family of alumni who have a common bond not unlike that which connects blood-kin. Wherever you go there go also our thoughts and our hopes for your continued growth and maturity and success in a spiritual sense.

And I pledge to you, on behalf of these, your faculty, our constant and continuing support in all your efforts. In return I ask your support, now and forevermore, of this university, your alma mater, in her constantly growing name and fame. I ask that you sustain her in her search for truth and the cause of orderly justice. I ask that you be loyal to her, if in the years ahead, she finds herself beleaguered by extremists of the left or of the right. Only if the University can count on you, her sons and daughters, to stand by her in times of trial, can her future be secure.

*(from Commencement Remarks,
University of Kentucky, May, 1969)*

FUTURE PLANS FOR THE UNIVERSITY OF KENTUCKY

Since receiving your letter of October 23, 1970, I have given some thought to the questions you raise and, as you suggested, I have consulted some friends both inside and outside the University. As a result, I have a few ideas that I will share with you. So that they may not seem too confused I shall arrange them in several categories without assigning priorities to any of them.

I. The Student Body

With rising costs and with little prospect of greatly increased appropriations or other income the University will be unable to continue the great expansion of faculty and staff it has experienced in the past decade. With bonding capacity also reaching its limit it will be impossible for the University to construct additional plants to accommodate more students. These two factors, it seems to me, should call for the University to reexamine its admission policies so as to freeze (perhaps that is too harsh a word) student enrollments at a pre-determined optimum level. Only in such a way, I would think, can the students who come here feel that it is possible that they may get adequate attention from their faculty.

Although the above policy would result in a static university insofar as King Numbers is concerned, it does not follow that the University must not grow qualitatively. On the contrary, wise decisions and proper planning now may permit the University to use the next decade for its most fruitful development.

But to successfully turn the University in the direction suggested would be quite revolutionary. It would, of course, meet with considerable opposition from many patrons of the University and from one end of the Commonwealth to the other. This opposition would have to be met with reason and with persuasive argument. Some arguments that might win converts can only be suggested:

1. With the present attrition rate of from one-third to one-half of the freshman class the state is providing plant and faculty at Lexington to conduct a vast screening program to weed out the large number of unqualified students who come here. This is a monstrous waste for the state as well as for the students who fail and their parents. The taxpayers should not be asked to foot such a bill, and the failing student and his parents should not be made to suffer the trauma that frequently must be attendant on such failure. It is better for the student never to have been admitted than to be brought here under conditions that point toward his failure. And the state should not and cannot afford such extravagant expenditures as the present admissions philosophy and policy entails. Fifty years ago, perhaps the relatively open admissions policy we now have might have been justified. At that time there was little or no alternative opportunity for the high school graduate of limited means and moderate ability than to enroll in his state university. But today, with the well equipped and reasonably well staffed regional universities and community colleges within commuting distance of most students, the marginal student does have a less-costly alternative to his state university.

2. If the above argument can be sustained, then it should be buttressed with an efficient screening of all applicants. Such a screening program should give reasonable assurance that only those applicants who have the ability *and the motivation* to successfully complete a four year program here would be admitted. Those about

whom there is doubt would have the opportunity of transferring here later, if they desired, after undergoing additional screening at one of the regional universities or community colleges.

3. Adoption of such a restrictive admissions policy as outlined above would call for a new philosophy on the part of our faculty. They should assume that *all* their students had already been adequately screened and were prepared to do the work expected of them. Instances of freshmen failure should be much less frequent than is now the case. And failures in his classes should cause deep concern to the individual professor. They might be regarded as *his* failure rather than failure by the student.

4. The selective admissions program would be received more enthusiastically if there could be created at the University an academic climate of such quality that students would feel that it was an opportunity and a privilege to win admission here.

5. As part of the screening process it should be recognized that some high school seniors possess unusual talents that cannot be measured by standardized achievement and intelligence tests. Such talents should be considered by admission officers, *provided* other evidence *predicts* that the student's native ability is such that he may be academically successful here. Such unusual talents might be in music, graphic arts, writing, debate, drama, or athletics.

6. A restricted admissions program might be better received throughout the state if the people in the geographical areas served by the community colleges would develop a pride in their college. Then students who for one reason or another found it advisable to enroll there would not feel that they were being relegated to a second-class institution. Indeed, the communities should be encouraged to recruit their best high school graduates into their transfer programs for the full two-year term. The University could do much to stimulate such a spirit in the several community college areas.

7. If there are University committees on which students properly should be represented but are not, this matter should be reexamined. I do not, however, favor student representation on committees reviewing matters of faculty tenure.

II. The Faculty

1. It is relatively easy to measure faculty competence in research; it is difficult to measure quality in teaching. I believe that more often

than not the good teacher is a productive researcher, and *vice versa.* But perhaps we have placed too little emphasis on teaching in our faculty reviews. Methods of evaluation should be evolved and records of teaching accomplishment accumulated in personnel files similar to those regarding other faculty activities.

2. In my opinion, the teaching load of faculty in many areas of the University are on the average too low. This may be the University's greatest area of extravagance. From my own experience I would say that a six hour teaching assignment for the faculty member who also has research duty is too light. In bygone days I taught two large classes (forty or more students each) every semester and in two of every three summer semesters while at the same time keeping office hours in an administrative post. At the same time I was able to maintain a consistent research program. While I would not recommend a return to such a Spartan schedule I believe almost any professor in an academic area should be able to teach three courses each semester.

3. Of course the University must remain competitive in faculty salaries and in fringe benefits. But still more needs to be done to attract superior faculty. As a dramatic move in this direction the University might launch a program for funds to endow a number of chairs.

III. Program

1. The recently completed self-study should be used to reexamine the University's programs and curricula. As a result of such a reexamination the University should be prepared to discontinue those programs that prove wasteful and unproductive. The great number of classes enrolling six or fewer students should be closely examined and made to justify their continuation.

2. It is well-known that too many students in the community colleges are enrolled in transfer programs and too few in terminal programs. Some of this is due to the failure to develop the terminal programs, and efforts need to be directed to their development. But perhaps, too, there has grown in the community colleges an impression that the transfer programs have a higher status than the terminal programs. If this is true, wiser counseling is called for in the community colleges as well as in the high schools of the state.

3. In cooperation with national agencies and other universities research should be undertaken looking to the compressing of the

time required for the completion both of undergraduate and graduate and professional programs. It needs to be demonstrated anew that a baccalaureate degree calls for 128 credit hours or that a Ph.D. program should call for four years of full time study.

4. In view of the employment opportunities it would seem that this University, like most others, has launched too many Ph.D. programs and that too many students have been enrolled in them. I believe that the time is ripe now to be highly selective in accepting students into these programs. It is becoming an exercise in frustration now for our current Ph.D. graduates to find teaching positions in higher education. More selective admissions would abate this frustration and would at the same time raise the quality level of our graduate student body.

These, A. D., are some of my thoughts on decisions that need to be made now or in the near future by the University. I apologize for the great length of this document. I had no idea when I started that I would be so long-winded.

*(in answer to a letter from A. D. Albright,
vice president for institutional planning—November 18, 1970)*

NOT A MAN OF BOUNDLESS PATIENCE

It is, indeed, an honor to participate in these exercises this evening when his fellow workers and neighbors, come together to honor and to express their affection for Herman Donovan and his lovely lady. There are, however, one or two things one must, in this situation, guard against. In the first place, one must not take oneself too seriously. That way lies boredom. I have been told that Mark Twain one day found himself cornered by such a serious minded individual and was unable to escape. After many clichés the bore finally made the earth-shaking observation that every time he drew breath some poor mortal died. "Have you," asked the exasperated humorist, "ever tried using cloves?" Now I hope that it will not be the destiny of any of you in this company to shuffle off this mortal coil during the next ten or fifteen minutes; but if that should be your fate I trust it will not be as the result of my—shall we say, exhalations.

A second course to avoid in affairs of this kind, I think, is the creation of a sombre atmosphere. Too often when a person has completed a phase of his career and is being honored for a job well done, his colleagues pull out all the nostalgic stops and speak as if he were leaving for the next world on the midnight limited. This is certainly not the spirit of this occasion. Actually, Herman Donovan has passed through one phase of his career and is beginning on a richer and more pleasant, and more fruitful one—that of the scholar. He gives promise of being a successful man. In the high office he has just laid aside he has borne himself well. He has been tried, figuratively, by ordeal of fire—not once but many a time. I know, because I was singed in some of them myself. Those of us who have watched him develop here over the past fifteen years into a top-flight executive and leader will be watching him with equal interest in the next fifteen, to see if he will become an equally fine scholar and writer. As I say, we have hopes for him. I would suggest that he reacts best to challenge and irritants. He needs something, occasionally, like a legislative investigation, or a challenge to his authority or to the University's integrity by some outside influence. If he can have something like that now and then, he'll go far.

A third thing I would avoid on this occasion is an inclination to gild the lily. Eulogisms and panegyrics may do well enough for funeral orations. Such, like too many biographies of great men, give a distorted picture—a picture out of focus—all spirit, with no flesh, and bone, and blood. We are not honoring a departed soul here tonight, but a dynamic, a very human, a vigorous man. I haven't consulted him about what I am going to say about him, but if I had I think he would have replied like Othello, "Speak of me as I am; nothing extenuate, nor set down aught in malice."

To begin with, then, Herman Donovan is *not* a man of boundless patience, I think it was Kipling's Tommy Atkins who made the observation that "single men in barracks don't grow into plaster saints." I believe it is equally true that lonely men in university president's offices don't either. And the first erosion that takes place in a personality as a result of the constant tug-of-war of conflicting forces trying to pull him this way and that, is likely to be in his equanimity.

I shall never forget one incident several years ago—trivial to insignificance in itself—which illustrates so aptly many things about Herman Donovan. I'm sure he never remembered this incident an hour after. It was budget-making time, and budget-making time in the president's office is something akin to sugar-making time on a Louisiana plantation, where all hands work twenty hours out of the twenty-four for a period of several weeks. Throughout the day, and day after day, the president sits at the long table in his office, with Leo Chamberlain at his right hand and Frank Peterson at his left: and the several deans, one by one, are called before this august trinity, than which, in the words of Guy Stanton Ford, there is no *whicher,* there to defend their budgets.

It was a late afternoon when I went in. I could see that the president had had a difficult day and that his patience had been strained. We quickly went over some routine items, and then we came to one concerning the percentage of salary to be paid an employee who was getting a change of work assignment. The question is much too complex to go into here. Suffice to say that my position was right and the president thought his was. We went round and round, the president maintaining I was trying to pay a larger salary than the man was entitled to. Finally, he lost patience completely, pounded his fist on the table and said "I'm not going to approve it! I'm not going to approve it!" Well, I am not exactly a Job-like person, myself, and besides I had had a tough day too. So I pounded right back at him, and said, "He's entitled to it! He's entitled to it!" We finally agreed to settle that question by conference between Frank and me, and then quickly went over the remaining items. Down at the bottom of the list I had modestly placed my own name suggesting the same salary that I received the year before. When the president came to this he drew his red-pencil through the figure and wrote in a much handsomer sum. Well, I was touched, and at the same time I hadn't completely cooled off. I said, "Mr. President, I rather thought you were going to fire me, but instead you raise my salary." "By George!" he replied, "if you pay out any money you shouldn't, I will fire you!"

This, as I have said, was a trivial and inconsequential incident; but it reflects, I think, so much of the personality of the man—his little human irritation at being crossed when he was positive he was right, and his quaint and negative way of indicating to me that he had confidence in my probity and in my judgment; his scrupulous adherence to policy; his attention to detail.

But what of the bigger events? What of the really consequential things which rolled by in an unending series year after year during the decade and a half that he guided the destinies of this institution? What are the things that will stand out and will endure? What are the really big contributions that this great and good man has made to this institution, to this community, and to the Commonwealth?

Impressive, of course, is the growth of the physical plant during the last ten years. Two men's and two women's residence halls; temporary and now permanent quarters for hundreds of married students and their families; a modern service building; a fine arts building second to none; a journalism building; a pharmacy building and a coliseum dedicated to the promotion not only of physical culture, but of great music and drama as well—these are things which will long stand as evidence of his wise and stable leadership.

But I would remember, more than this, his wisdom some eight years ago when integration came to our campus. Through his firmness and fairness and good sense the explosive incidents which have occurred too many other places have been avoided here. I would remember, too, that more than anything else, more than all his buildings, his primary concern has been for the welfare of his faculty. He has struggled with governor after governor and legislature after legislature, and with considerable success, persuading them to give him funds to build up, and care for, and keep a constantly growing and improved faculty. His sustaining of the faculty has not been economic alone. He has been their staunch defender on the few occasions when their loyalty has been questioned. He has insisted on the right of academic freedom; on their right to participate in political issues; even on their right to stand for office, if they chose. He has publicized and praised their achievements; he has raised their prestige.

I think I shall remember too, the tenseness and anxiety and excitement that was an incident of every commencement exercise which Herman Donovan conducted. Anyone can follow a printed program. But Herman Donovan didn't believe in anything as prosaic as that. The chorus might rehearse long hours for the brief rendition it was to give. They might be listed on the program first, but only Herman Donovan knew whether they would sing first, last, in the middle—or, in fact, whether they would sing at all. The several deans had been carefully schooled on their appearances as to time and substance. But this meant nothing when Donovan was at the lectern and running the show. And so the deans sighed with relief when degrees were awarded to their candidates. Yet despite the thrill the pilot gave his crew he always safely brought his ship to port. No planned note of music ever went unsung, no distinguished guest ever failed of recognition, and no qualified candidate ever failed to receive his degree "with all the rights and privileges pertaining thereto."

I would remember that Herman Donovan has on many occasions, and sometimes under trying circumstances, maintained the independence and the integrity of the University, when its freedom or its good name was under attack.

And, finally, I would remember, in this day when friction and misunderstanding between faculties and regents is so common—even among our greater universities—when mistrust between town and gown has reached dangerous proportions—that Herman Donovan has cultivated confidence and respect between this university's faculty and its trustees which is in great contrast to what has been going on at Berkeley and Los Angeles, at Seattle, at Illinois, and Michigan, Ohio State. This confidence was most recently fortified and cemented when the trustees requested advice and help from the faculty in the selection of a new president. And the fruit of that cooperative effort has resulted, most happily, in the selection of a young man of great ability, of great courage and charm—one who has the respect, and confidence, and loyal support of every member of this faculty.

These are the things I shall remember about Herman Donovan's administration. Most of them are intangibles, but they may endure long after the steel and stone of Fine Arts and Coliseum are rubble. They were won only through his great skill, his great wisdom, and his unbounded courage. And it is because of these that we here can say tonight, "Here is a man! When comes another?"

(from Donovan Retirement Banquet Speech, 1956)

YOU MADE US WHAT WE ARE TODAY

For a number of years now, Phi Alpha Theta has been holding these annual dinner meetings. Tonight, however, this is no ordinary occasion; for we are coming to the end of an era in this little world of ours, the Department of History at the University of Kentucky.

As all by this time must know, the University has reorganized its academic structure so that where we formerly had department heads whose tenure was indefinite and under ordinary circumstances permanent, we now have chairmen who are appointed for a fixed period, normally for four years. In the future, the rotation of a chairman will be a routine event, not one to make ceremonious, a mere changing of the guard, so to speak. But our present chairman will retire from that office (although not from the department, praise God) at the end of the present year. And this is a special affair, for he has held office as department head for almost a quarter of a century. And without his knowledge or consent, his colleagues have determined that they will not let him slip out of his seat of power without confronting him with the record of his administration, and they have deputized me to present the evidence to you. To this end, we have drawn up a bill of particulars and propose to dissect and analyze his administration. And when you have heard this, I am sure that you will agree with me that the evidence will support the conviction we have reached concerning him, so that it would be useless for him to attempt to refute the charges. Accordingly, we have allowed no time for him to speak after me.

I was here at the University, although in an unrelated field of endeavor, when Tom Clark assumed leadership of the history department. He was a young man, then, not long out of the Mississippi prairie country, a young man with unbounded self-confidence, yet with a sense of deep humility; one with an almost superhuman capacity of work and concentration, yet with an effervescent good humor and overpowering sense of comedy. He took charge of a department which hardly deserved the name. . . .

When I was a boy, many years ago, there was an old lyric that runs through my memory tonight. It was a haunting melody with an accusative refrain, a lament, I think, of a rejected lover. It went something like this: "You made me what I am today; I hope you're satisfied." And it is in that mood and in that spirit, that we, the present members of the department and heirs to those who went before us, turn to our retiring chairman and repeat that old melody: "You made us what we are today: we hope you're satisfied."

And what has happened to that department over which he assumed leadership twenty-five years ago? Has it developed as a well-led department should? Has it grown, not only in size, but in maturity, and wisdom, and stature? Has it ranged beyond the somewhat narrow limits which were its academic boundaries then?

Insofar as size is concerned the evidence is here before you; it has grown more than threefold, to 19½ members here on the Lexington campus alone, together with numerous other colleagues in the neighboring community colleges. You might be interested to know how I arrived at this figure of 19½. I first attempted to ascertain the number of staff by counting the offices and multiplying by 2, but I found this wouldn't work because there are many more than twice as many staff as there are offices. I then counted desks, but this wouldn't work either, because several people share desks: so I ended by counting offices, desks, desk-drawers, and then computing by a complicated formula, which I will not bother you with.

Areas of specialization of this expanded department are widespread with Ancient, Medieval, Far East, Russian, Latin-American specialists in addition to the more traditional areas, and with budgetary allotments for two other positions, one of whom I believe will be a specialist in the Near or Middle East.

In this respect then, that of growth in numbers, I think that we will have to conclude that the chairman's administration has been a success story. Probably no other department in this university has experienced a similar growth.

But what has this greatly enlarged department accomplished, other than to teach and complain about classes too large and offices too small? In the twenty years since the chairman began adding to his staff, men he has recruited have published thirty-eight books, seven in the last year and with several additional manuscripts now in the final stages of preparation. This is more than the rest of the College of Arts and Sciences has produced during the same period, and it is many more than the combined faculties of the colleges of Law, Engineering, Agriculture, Education, and Commerce have produced. Other departments count publications by the article; this one counts them by volumes. Members of his department have held six Guggenheim Fellowships, nine Fulbright Fellowships; four have been elected Distinguished Professor of the Year in the College of Arts and Sciences, two have served as lecturers at the Salzburg Seminar, three have held Ford Fellowships, one has been elected to the Pitt Professorship of History at Cambridge University, four have won Alumni Research Awards.

As an outsider, or at least only half a member of the department, I think it is not improper for me to run over this tale, counting these accomplishments. It is a record of which not only this department can be proud, but one in which all members of the University community may well take pride. On the score of quality and maturity and scholarship then, I think we will have to agree that this chairman, soon to become an exchairman, has acquitted himself with credit.

But what of his personal record? Has he kept up with the fast pace of the men he has brought in? Just who is this chairman of the department of history at the University of Kentucky? Who is Tom Clark? He is many different people. Ask the publishing houses of the country and they will tell you that he is one of the profession's most prolific and most distinguished members, author of ten books which have been distinctive contributions to the history of the South and of the American Frontier, and that he has also edited the rich six-volume travel series of the South. Ask the Guggenheim Foundation, and they will tell you that he is one of their fellows. Ask the Fulbright Commission, the Salzburg Seminar, Oxford University, the United States State Department, and they will tell you that he has been one of their most distinguished lecturers. Ask any member of the faculty of this University and he will tell you that Tom Clark is one of the first men they selected as Distinguished Professor, the first person that they elected as their representative on the Board of Trustees, one of the faculty committee of four they elected to choose a president two years ago. Ask any member of the history profession "Who is Tom Clark?" and they will tell you he is a former president of the Southern Historical Association, a past national President of Phi Alpha Theta, former president of the Mississippi Valley [Historical Association] and chairman of its executive committee for a longer term than any other man save one. Ask Phi Beta Kappa who he is and they will tell you he is one of their speakers who is most in demand to address its many chapters.

I think you will agree with me, then, that the record indicates that our chairman has built this, the strongest department in this University, and one of the truly distinguished history departments in the country, at a time when he has himself been setting the pace, establishing a reputation for himself as one of the most eminent of the country's historians.

What then of the future? One might fear that such a man as I have described would be irreplaceable, and that any department losing such leadership must needs slip from the pinnacle to which he had brought it. We do not think so. If that should come to pass, then he would not have builded as firmly as we now know he has. And it is because he has brought such people as Carl Cone into his department that we have no fear for the future. Rather it is a measure of Tom's true greatness, that we look forward with unbounded confidence to even greater development of the department and its program under Carl's leadership.

And so, Tom, in recognition of your remarkable contributions to this department, of your service to the University, the Commonwealth, the nation, and the profession, I am privileged to announce that your colleagues have chosen you Theodore Hallam Professor for the next two years. But the department has done more than that. The department has elected several persons to the Hallam Professorship; this time the Professorship is designated as a Chair. And so that there may be no misunderstanding of this, your colleagues are presenting you with a chair. It was too large to bring here, but it has been delivered to your home, and when you return there tonight you will find it in your study. I'm not sure whether it is a rocking chair or a swivel chair, but I want you to know that it is the Hallam Chair. And in the coming years, when you will no longer have to be burdened with administering the details of the department, we want you to just sit in it and relax and reflect. And with every rock or with every turn, according to the nature of the chair, you will know that you have the gratitude and the deep affection of all your colleagues.

(from speech at Phi Alpha Theta Banquet honoring Thomas D. Clark's tenure as chairman of the University of Kentucky history department, April 1968)

STATEMENT BEFORE EXECUTIVE COMMITTEE OF SOUTHEASTERN CONFERENCE

As I understand the conditions under which we are here, as outlined in President [John] Gallalee's letter, we are not to discuss the question of Kentucky's guilt of the charges that have been brought against her. That question has already been determined by the

Committee and even though we are in disagreement, we are not permitted to argue that matter further. The only question to be discussed and considered here is whether or not the penalty [suspension of Kentucky's basketball team for the 1952-53 season] – imposed by the Committee at our hearing a month ago and announcement of which has been withheld pending this appeal–is excessive. I shall confine my remarks to that issue.

To give you gentlemen a more complete picture of conditions prevailing in the Conference over a long period of time, I think it would not be inappropriate for me to refer to specific instances of rule violations in the past of which I have particular knowledge. Let me assure you before doing so that I mention these instances with no intention of preferring charges against any other institution. I mention them only in order to demonstrate that Kentucky's violations are not of such a peculiarly aggravated nature as to warrant the severe penalty which you are considering imposing upon her.

Ten years ago I was a coach in this Conference. I had been a very successful high school coach in Louisville. Wally Butts was coach at another high school in Louisville at that same time, President [O. C.] Aderholt, and I was able to hold my own with him. I suppose I had better teams than he had in those high school days. But I was not able to hold my own with him, or with other coaches, after we came into the Conference. I make no pretentions that I was a good coach, but for one reason or another, perhaps because of my inferior ability but I choose to think there were other causes, I was not a successful coach at Kentucky.

We broke no rules while I was coaching at Kentucky. We had only sixty scholarships in football at that time, forty varsity and twenty freshmen. We not only broke no rules in awarding grants-in-aid, we did not even grant the full scholarship permitted. We gave only board, room, books and institutional fees at Kentucky at that time. We gave not a cent to any athlete for laundry or for any other purpose. And yet I had many opportunities to do so. Frequently sports fans came to me with offers of money to make illegitimate inducements to promising athletes to enroll at Kentucky, but I spurned all such overtures. I claim no particular credit for having done so. I am one of those unfortunate people with a tender conscience–I even observe speed limit signs along the highways. I am unable to enjoy any peace or happiness whenever I think I have done anything illegal.

But what conditions did prevail in the Conference at that time in that respect? In general we had the same Conference rules then as now with only a few alterations in recent years. But these rules were uniformly broken by coaches then as now.

I remember sitting in a room in this hotel ten years ago at a gathering of coaches. Frank Thomas, President Gallalee, Major [Robert] Neyland and Dean [N. W.] Dougherty were laughingly discussing a controversy they had over a football player named Tommy O'Brien. Tommy was a great high school football player in Montgomery who was eagerly sought by many schools. Frank Thomas offered him—through Dr. [Skip] Blue, an Alabama alumnus in Montgomery, $7,500 cash, plus a full scholarship for himself and his sister, but Tennessee got him because they met this offer and threw in a scholarship for Tommy's bride and an apartment for them to live in. They discussed this incident quite frankly and quite humorously in my presence and in the presence of others, and Frank Thomas later told me in all sincerity that the incident had actually developed just as outlined in their conversation.

It was at about that time that the Conference had just chosen its first Commissioner, Mike Connor. Conner had a meeting of all the coaches and athletic directors in the dining room of this hotel. He had called us all together to ask us to pledge ourselves to obey the conference rules. One by one we all stood up and said we would obey the rules, until it came Dudy Noble's time, your athletic director, President [F. T.] Mitchell. Mr. Noble stood up and said he would not obey the rules and he didn't think anyone else would. "Until three years ago," said Noble, "we obeyed every rule and what did it get us? We finished at the bottom of the Conference year after year. Since that time there isn't a rule in the book we haven't broken and where are we now. This year we're playing in the Orange Bowl."

It was at the same time that Dudy Noble gave me what he thought was good advice for a young coach. It was a friendly act and I do not mention it to discredit him, for I have great respect for his basic honesty according to his code. But he told me to use what money I could raise to "buy" good backs. Linemen, he said, could be made but backs could not, and the good ones come at a premium. But, he said, the price was not always prohibitive, and he pointed out that Bill Black, the star of the Mississippi State team that year, had cost him only $500 above the legitimate scholarship.

It was about this time, too, that a boy by the name of Hubert

Schurtz, of Pinckneyville, Illinois, had accepted a scholarship at Kentucky. We had a rule then, as now, that a freshman could not report at the school until September 1, and a Kentucky alumnus at a nearby town, Duquoin, had promised to drive the boy down to Kentucky on that date. But ten days before, this alumnus called me and told me that Schurtz had been picked up by the freshman coach of L.S.U. and was in Baton Rouge. I immediately protested to Commissioner Connor. Connor investigated and reported that the boy was not in Baton Rouge but was visiting at the camp of a "friend" outside the city, and he did not see, under the circumstances, that he could do anything about it because the boy was not on the L.S.U. campus. So Schurtz stayed on at L.S.U. and played football there until he entered the service. The head football coach at L.S.U. then was our present Commissioner, Bernie Moore.

Now, let me repeat, I am not relating these events of a decade ago in order to embarrass you gentlemen whose institutions were at fault, nor am I bringing charges against your institutions. I merely recount them to show you what was going on in the Conference at that time and for many years before, without the knowledge of you gentlemen, I am sure.

Well, you may say, that was all true years ago. What goes on now? Let us look and see what the situation is now.

We have the sworn statement of a boy from Springfield, Ohio, a boy named [Dick] Shatto, that he was offered $3,000 to enroll at Auburn, and $5,000 to enroll at Georgia—or it may be the other way around, $5,000 at Auburn and $3,000 at Georgia. And in that regard I should mention what I consider a remarkable conclusion the Commissioner has reached in this case. He has told me that he thinks he will declare the boy ineligible at Kentucky because—

(Mr. Moore interrupted to say that the reason he contemplated such a ruling was that the boy had been paid excessive traveling expenses while visiting Auburn and Tennessee. Mr. Kirwan resumed)

Exactly what I was going to say. And I think it an amazing procedure for the Commissioner to take when there is no evidence that the boy was seduced by the illegitimate offer. Let me show you what confusion such a policy can get us into. Let us assume that Tennessee has signed up a prospect whom Kentucky is seeking. Kentucky could invite the boy for a visit, and while there, the boy might be offered $15.00 or $20.00 in excess of his actual traveling expenses. It would be an easy way for Kentucky to obtain the disqualification of many of Tennessee's best prospects. I contend that we should be punished in such a case, not the boy and not Tennessee.

I call your attention, too, to a remarkable phrase the Commissioner just used. You heard him say he might rule the boy ineligible because he was paid "excessive traveling expenses." Actually the rules forbid the payment of any traveling expenses and any payment should be punished. This is a rule of both our Conference and of the N.C.A.A. It is more than a rule. It is a solemn compact which we entered into with the Eastern Intercollegiate Athletic Association at Dallas two years ago. The year before that, the N.C.A.A. had nearly expelled Virginia, V.P.I., the Citadel, and several other schools for not adhering to the Sanity Code. We were not adhering to the Sanity Code either and neither were any of you. I spoke against the Sanity Code as the representative of the S.E.C. at that Dallas meeting. I don't know whether any of you gentlemen were present or not—yes, you were there Dean Dougherty. I told that gathering that I could not vote for the expulsion of members who were not overemphasizing athletics nearly so much as were we. V.P.I. was about to be expelled for overemphasizing athletics when they had not won a game in three years, while we were given a clear bill of health after playing in two major bowls in the past two years. They had answered a questionnaire truthfully while we and you had resorted to subterfuge.

Well, I say this rule about paying traveling expenses is a sacred compact. For at that Dallas meeting, we of the S.E.C. were engaged in a crusade to eliminate the Sanity Code. At the same time, the Eastern Association was intent upon obtaining the passage of the Dartmouth Amendment which forbade the payment of such expenses. And so we had a meeting with representatives of the Eastern Association—I was a member of our group who consulted with them. And at that conference, they promised to vote with us to outlaw the Sanity Code if we would vote for the Dartmouth Amendment and obey the Amendment if it passed. And together we secured our joint aims. Several months later our Conference met and wrote the Dartmouth Amendment into our own rules.

Now at that very meeting our coaches held a meeting to set up machinery to void the Dartmouth Amendment. Almost at the same time, we were passing the Amendment to make it unlawful for a school to pay the traveling expenses of prospective athletes to visit member institutions, our coaches were meeting in another room where they agreed to set up dummy agencies to pay such expenses. And now every institution in this Conference has such an agency which violates this rule for them. Is that not true, Commissioner?

(Commissioner Moore said he thought it was "probably" true, but he could not prove it.)

Do you say "probably," Commissioner? (Commissioner Moore repeated that he could not prove it was true.)

Did you not sit in the room with the coaches, Commissioner, and advise with them as to how they could best achieve their objective?

(The Commissioner admitted that he had.)

I might say, gentlemen, that I have given positive instructions to our coaches that in the future all rules must be obeyed by Kentucky —even those which are universally condoned like this one.

(The Commissioner observed that he thought it would not be a violation, provided the expenses were not paid directly by the school.)

But that is the very practice for which we were told we would have to answer for permitting citizens of Lexington to make cash payments to our players. We were told here a month ago that if Mr. Rupp had made the request for tournament expense money for players to the University Athletic Association, and if the Athletic Association had approved and made the payments out of University funds, such procedure would not be considered in violation of rules. Now we are told by the Commissioner that if we let an outside agency act for us in another rule evasion, it is all right.

Be that as it may, violation of this rule is universal. I have a statement from a boy from Ashland, Kentucky, President [J. H.] Miller, to the effect that John Mauer, your basketball coach personally handed him money for round-trip plane travel to Gainesville. I have a statement from a boy from Western Kentucky to the effect that Cliff Wells, basketball coach at Tulane, handed him money for a round-trip fare to New Orleans. I have a statement from a boy in Scottsboro, Alabama, Dean Dougherty, charging that he was worked out by Coach Lowery in Knoxville in violation of Conference rules. These are all violations of our Conference rules, of N.C.A.A. rules, and of the solemn gentleman's agreement we made with the Eastern Association. And these violations are condoned and the procedure of the violation was worked out with the approval of the Commissioner.

Nothing could emphasize more than the Commissioner's latest remark the hopeless confusion in which the Conference and the coaches find themselves. Some rules can be violated and nothing will come of it. Other rules must be obeyed. Which rules fall in each category? That is a question which, apparently, each coach must figure out for himself, and I must confess that I am in considerable doubt as to how to advise them.

Now, gentlemen, it is my personal opinion that athletics are overemphasized at all of our institutions. If I had my way, Kentucky would have given its last athletics scholarship. I think the scholarship is a travesty and a joke. I think it has merely placed a floor under aid to athletes. All of them get that, then those who can demand more—some $200 like [Chester] Lukawski, some $7,500 like Tommy O'Brien.

Yet we are placed in the position, because of all this confusion, of deciding which rules must be obeyed and which can be violated with impunity. This means that we must classify rules as good and bad—or rather as bad and not-so-bad.

How are we to arrive at such a determination? It is immoral, it seems to me, to deliberate on a question of what laws to break. Nevertheless, since the decision has to be made, let's tackle it.

In my opinion, if one type of rule violation is worse than another—if I have to decide what violations are particularly immoral—I would say that those violations which bribe a boy to enroll in a particular institution are most immoral. Such things as the offering Tommy O'Brien $7,500, President Gallalee and Dean Dougherty. Such violations as the paying $500 to Bill Black, President Mitchell. At the same time, I would call your attention to the fact that all the violations of which we are charged—with the exception of the one case of Lukawski which we have confessed—were not of this nature. There is not a scintilla of evidence pointing to any other conclusion. The record shows that Groza, Beard, and Spivey were all enrolled in Kentucky for more than a year before the illegal subsidies were paid them. These offenses, it seems to me, are of less grievousness by great odds than the charge I have just made against Auburn and Georgia in the case of the Shatto boy of Springfield, Ohio.

Nor is the Shatto incident an isolated instance. On the contrary, it conforms to a pattern that I am sure is characteristic not only of this Conference but of many other institutions as well. The Commissioner knows this is true for he and I have discussed it together on several occasions. As recently as last December at New Orleans we discussed it. I was worried about the problem and so was he, and he told me at that time that coaches were bidding so extravagantly for players that he didn't know what would become of the Conference. Now he tells me that he can find no evidence of rules evasion other than at Kentucky. What, I ask him, has become of the evidence he seemed to be possessed of in New Orleans last winter?

But it may be that I am wandering too far afield in bringing up all these vexing and confusing incidents. Yet I think they logically belong in a consideration of whether or not the punishment you have indicated you may inflict on Kentucky is excessive. For they demonstrate, I think beyond all doubt, that Kentucky's violations are not, in comparison, of such a heinous nature as to bar us from associating with nice people like yourselves, and of letting our students play games with your students.

So far as I know, the punishment which you contemplate is without precedent in American intercollegiate athletics. Never, to my knowledge, has an institution been forbidden to engage in sport. Even the Southern Conference, in the cases of Maryland and Clemson, permitted the violators to play outside the Conference, and barred them only from play within the Conference. Yet, Maryland's and Clemson's offense, it seems to me, was far greater than Kentucky's. For those two institutions not only broke a Conference rule but they also defied the Conference. Virtually, when they were called to task after they accepted their bowl invitations, they told the Conference to "go to hell." Kentucky has not defied the S.E.C. We have been negligent. That is the extent of our institutional guilt. When we found that rules had been violated at Kentucky, we called you in, told you all we knew and asked for just punishment. We did not want and have not asked for a whitewash.

President Donovan mentioned a few minutes ago that suspension of our basketball team from all competition would constitute fining us in the amount of $100,000, since our net income would be reduced by that amount. As a matter of fact Mr. Shively, our Athletics Director, informs me that as nearly as he can compute, the figure would be $103,000. If you were to formally impose such a fine, the world would be shocked at such severity. Yet, I would be willing to pay a much larger sum if by doing so we could wash ourselves clean of this whole sordid affair. We have in our Athletics

Association treasury a surplus of a quarter million dollars. I would be willing to pay all this, I would eagerly pay two and one-half times this suggested fine, if by doing so, I could avoid all the fanfare of publicity which this basketball scandal has brought upon us.

The real punishment that the University of Kentucky has had imposed on it is the humiliation and shame attendant upon its involvement in the basketball fix scandal, and the glaring and searching publicity, emanating principally from the New York press but copied from coast to coast and from Michigan to the Gulf. We have been convicted before the people of America as a conscienceless and immoral institution which admits athletes who are not qualified, whose faculty condones cribbing of athletes, and whose coach exploits them to the complete disregard of their moral and physical welfare. Nor have they stopped with indictments of our University officials and faculty. Our alumni, our trustees and the townspeople of our community are all brought into the sweeping denunciation of the New York judge. Nor are you gentlemen immune from Judge Streit's unreasoned charges. Each of your institutions and each of you as president is included in this all-embracing indictment.

When the Commissioner was in Lexington making his investigation, I urged him to look into these other charges—those which strike at the very integrity of the institution—and say whether or not they were true. His position then was, and perhaps rightly, that this was an athletics conference and that these other charges were not within the jurisdiction of this body. It is because of these charges that I would pay any amount of money if by so doing we could vindicate our name.

Now I know, gentlemen, that you are not trying us for the basketball fix, and I do not want you to think I am here belaboring this point—beating a dead horse. Yet, in the public mind suspending us from the conference will convict our faculty, our trustees, and our officials of all of Judge Streit's outlandish charges.

It is this which constitutes our real punishment—not the loss of $100,000 or any sum. Our faculty is in a state of ferment. Three different faculty committees are at work investigating our athletics situation. They are demoralized. They don't know what to believe or to disbelieve. We have lost more faculty members to other institutions this year than in any previous year. Our student body is demoralized, and there is no doubt but that our enrollment will suffer sharply as a result of this very unfavorable publicity.

This humiliation is our real punishment. This publicity has dogged us now for nine months—ever since the first of the boys were arrested last October. That event, of course, brought glaring headlines; then the boys were brought back to Kentucky—more headlines; then they were ... tried but not sentenced—more headlines; then they were taken again to New York and sentenced—and still more headlines.

If action now could bring this matter to a close, we could start now the long and slow process of rehabilitating our name as an educational institution. People forget quickly, though this event will live long in their memories. But if we could come to the end of this now, our shame would drop out of the news and in time it would be only a tragic memory.

But if we are suspended for a year, our humiliation will be prolonged throughout the next twelve months and thereafter. There will be reference to us in the press every time a basketball game is played and Kentucky does not play, and our guilt will be perpetuated before the public. This, gentlemen, is needless persecution. We have already suffered all the penalty any institution can endure. It is time to let us start our long road back. To prolong our shame is indeed the flogging of a dead horse. It is needless persecution.

President Donovan mentioned a minute ago that the U. S. Constitution forbids "cruel and inhuman punishment." I am aware that this Committee is not inhibited by any constitutional restrictions, but there is another provision in the same Constitution that I would call to your attention. Section 10 of Article 1 forbids a state to pass a law or impose a penalty which would alter the terms of a contract. We have contracts to play Notre Dame and several other schools. You have the power to make us cancel these games, because if we disregard your verdict—a thing we have no inclination to do—you can expel us from the Conference. But I merely call your attention to the fact that each of you, as an official and agent of your state, is exercising a power greater and more far reaching than your state legislature could exercise.

And finally, gentlemen, while I am no criminologist or even psychologist, I believe that the philosophy of punishment is impregnated with rehabilitation. Even the relatively impersonal courts temper justice with mercy in the hope that the criminal may then be induced to reform. Even the relatively alien—insofar as Kentucky and the section are concerned—New York Court showed such mercy to Groza and Beard and Barnstable when they appeared before it.

The University of Kentucky is not a criminal institution. We have been negligent in not exercising as close supervision over our athletics program as we know now we should. But we will not make that mistake again. We are impressed with the seriousness of our predicament. Our coaches are impressed and mean henceforth to abide by the rules regardless of what penalty you impose on us. Before coming down here I informed them that in the future they must obey all the rules, even the Dartmouth Amendment which is universally violated. They will obey this rule even though its observance places them at a great disadvantage with their rivals.

I have perhaps spoken more frankly than I should have and it may be that my case will suffer as a result of my frankness. But, gentlemen, I felt it my duty to enlighten you in regard to the situation in the Conference—conditions of hopeless confusion in rule observance—conditions of which I had particular knowledge and which I am sure you did not have.

And so, gentlemen, I close with this promise. If you will permit us to start now to rehabilitate ourselves I pledge you my word of honor as a gentleman, that if Kentucky violates the law again, the guilty person—be he who he may—will have to go—or I will go.

CIVIL WAR HISTORY

King Cotton   115

The Whole Union is Our Country   116

Toward the Abyss   118

Without Due Process   126

The Kentucky Soldier in the Civil War   127

The Orphan Brigade   129

How Did the People Keep Body
and Soul Together   131

The Gates to a Future   134

KING COTTON

An agricultural revolution had occurred in the ante-bellum South through the development of cotton culture. In the late eighteenth century, when South Carolina was its focal point, 50,000 bales of 300 pounds each had been the annual crop. From this modest beginning the culture had spread so that by 1860 it was the chief staple from North Carolina to Texas. Decade after decade, production increased in geometric proportion. The crop in 1860 was the biggest ever: that year 4,000,000 bales of 500 pounds were harvested. It was a soil-depleting crop, and in a day when extensive fertilization and crop rotation were uncommon, required new lands for survival. As production increased, the price of cotton declined; even so, there were quick profits to be made from it so long as new land was available. It was cotton that lured settlers from the Upper to the Lower South, and it was cotton that rejuvenated the South's "peculiar institution" at a time when slavery was proving unprofitable in the older section.

Before the Civil War the value of the cotton crop was not only greater than any other exported from the United States but also exceeded the value of all others combined. But when war threatened it was not the money value of the white fluffy staple that loomed largest with Southern politicians. They thought of it as an economic weapon to win diplomatic victories both in the North and in Europe. About one-fourth of the annual crop was consumed in the textile mills of the Northern states, where cotton manufacturing was the dominant industry. Most of the remainder of the crop was shipped to England, where it supplied the Lancashire looms with three-fourths of their raw product and engaged the services of nearly a million operatives. It has been estimated that about one-fifth of England's population at the time was directly dependent upon the cotton industry and that finished cotton goods comprised from two-fifths to one-half of the country's exports. The remainder of the cotton crop was shipped to France and Belgium. It was not nearly so important to their economies as to Britain's, yet France consumed more than 600,000 bales in 1860, most of it imported from America, and stoppage of this supply would bring distress to tens of thousands of workers.

Knowledge of these facts gave Southerners a supreme confidence in the invulnerability of the Confederacy. It was unthinkable that businessmen and statesmen of the world would suffer any interruption of their supply of cotton. If war should come, surely every Southerner could dispose of seven Yanks, but how could war come? Northern businessmen would never permit it. And even if they should fail to prevent war, Great Britain and France would intervene and put a stop to it. The world could not survive without cotton.

(from The Confederacy, *pp. 225-26)*

THE WHOLE UNION IS OUR COUNTRY

Kentucky's attachment for the Union had undergone great change in the half century since James Wilkinson's flirtation with the Spanish governor at New Orleans. In 1828 Crittenden had been one of a legislative committee that replied to South Carolina's Exposition and Protest against the Tariff. Four years later he was speaker of the house when the legislature by a unanimous vote declared South Carolina's nullification ordinance "contrary to the constitution and . . . destructive to the peace and harmony of the Union." The years had brought, if anything, closer ties between Kentucky and the Union. Thomas B. Stevenson, who was in Frankfort during the winter of 1848-1849, thought no one, Whig or Democrat, sympathized with secession. The Union, he added, "is valued above all estimation of slavery."

In his message to the legislature in 1848 Crittenden dwelt on Kentucky's stake in the Union. Her "dearest interests," he said, lay in its preservation. Its dissolution would remedy no ills but would be the *"consummation of the greatest evil that can befall us."* Kentucky, he concluded, would defend the Union to the utmost. In the year that followed, the crisis, instead of abating, deepened. By December, 1849, there were plans for a convention of slave states to decide upon a common policy looking to secession. The border states would be crucial. "Everything is to depend from this day on the course of Kentucky, Tennessee, and Missouri," wrote a Boston editor. Crittenden saw the danger. He was forewarned by friends in Washington, and he determined to speak even more bluntly against the secessionists than he had the year before.

His message to the legislature in December, 1849, was a well-reasoned discourse on constitutional theory. The Constitution, he said, was not the creature of the states, as Calhoun argued, but was made by the people. It was the highest law of the land, and "Inviolable respect and obedience" were due it. It both confirmed all the rights of the states and united "us . . . as one people." All states had pledged to abide by and support the Constitution and the Union it created.

Turning from theory to policy, he reiterated that Kentucky's material well-being was linked to the Union. The state's commercial ties with the Mississippi Valley, he said, were closer than with the gulf states. The great valley would never consent to destruction of the Union, which would close the Mississippi River to its exports. Self-interest, therefore, as well as nobler motives, made the Union a "necessity" to the Mississippi Valley and also to Kentucky. Kentucky sympathized with the southern states, but she would never harbor a thought against the Union and would abide by it to the last. "Dear as Kentucky is to us," he concluded, "she is not our whole country. The Union, the whole Union, is our country; and proud as we justly are of the name of *Kentuckian,* we have a loftier and more far-famed title—that of American Citizen."

It was a noble document, and the legislature gave it solid support. A senate resolution calling on all good citizens to cherish the Union and to denounce all efforts to break "the sacred ties which now . . . link together the various parts" passed by an overwhelming majority. How much the hands of Clay, Webster, Douglas, and other Unionists were strengthened in Washington by stout Unionist voices in Kentucky can only be conjectured. It is a fact, however, that Kentucky gave no encouragement to the Nashville convention in the spring and summer of 1850. And Crittenden played the leading part in aligning his state so solidly with the Union.

(from John J. Crittenden:
The Struggle for the Union, *pp. 245-46)*

TOWARD THE ABYSS

Despite Crittenden's plea for moderation, Wigfall of Texas made an incendiary speech on December 13, praising South Carolina for making preparations to secede. A few days later Ben Wade of Ohio responded, in a harsh and vindictive speech. He sneered at the petty insignificance of South Carolina, denied the right of secession, and predicted that Lincoln would use force against seceding states and that secessionists would eventually meet the fate of traitors. He renounced all talk of compromise as humiliating to Republicans.

Meanwhile, Crittenden had been carefully formulating what he hoped might be a final settlement of the slavery issue. All compromises on the question since 1787 had been mere legislative acts, subject to alteration by later congressional action. Thus the Missouri Compromise had been repealed by the Kansas-Nebraska Act, which sabotaged the peace so dearly won in 1850. Compromise agreements reached this time must be more permanent; they must be embodied in amendments to the Constitution itself. In preparing his plan, Crittenden consulted with friends from all sections. It was certain now that South Carolina would secede, but he hoped, as he had written Orlando Brown, that conciliatory measures might dissuade other states "from following her bad example."

On Wednesday, December 18, Crittenden arose in the Senate to present his proposals for compromise. They consisted of a series of unamendable amendments to the Constitution:

1. Restore the Missouri Compromise line (36°30') and extend it to California. Slavery, during the territorial stage, would be recognized south and prohibited north of the line. When states were created from the territories, they could come in as free or slave as they chose.
2. Prohibit Congress from abolishing slavery on government property in slave states.
3. Prohibit Congress from abolishing slavery in the District of Columbia so long as it existed in Maryland or Virginia. Even then it could not be done without consent of inhabitants or without compensation.
4. Prohibit Congress from interfering with the interstate transportation of slaves.
5. Compensate claimants of fugitive slaves rescued by mobs.
6. Prohibit future constitutional amendments that would (a) re-

duce the additional representation allowed states for three-fifths of their slaves, (b) alter the fugitive-slave requirement of the Constitution, or (c) give Congress power to interfere with slavery in the states.

The plan also called for a series of congressional resolutions:
1. The present fugitive-slave law was constitutional, should not be repealed, and ought to be enforced.
2. State laws conflicting with the act were null and void and ought to be repealed by the states.
3. Congress should amend the fugitive-slave law so as to delete certain clauses obnoxious to northern citizens.
4. Congress should strengthen and enforce laws prohibiting the foreign slave trade.

Crittenden explained that in preparing his proposals, he had looked impartially from section to section in order to seek out the causes of discontent as well as the means to remedy them. He did not regard his proposals as definitive, but he hoped that with amendments they might be made acceptable to the country. The question, he said, was not partisan; it was a question of the very life of the republic, "the life of this great people." He realized that northern men would find it difficult to sanction the legality of slavery south of the 36°30' line. Yet this was a mere trifle if it would prevent the breakup of the Union. The overthrow of the Union would be "the greatest shock that civilization and free government have received," more momentous in its consequences and "more fatal to mankind" even than the French Revolution. . . .

The failure of the Crittenden proposals in the Committee of Thirteen must be charged to its Republican members. Had Seward asked, when he returned to Washington on December 24, for a reconsideration of the vote on Crittenden's proposals, it is highly probable that Collamer and Doolittle would have joined him in voting for them. If so, the proposals would have passed the committee with at least eleven votes. Reported to the Senate by such a majority, they would have been brought to a speedy vote and approval there, probably by a constitutional majority. The House then, with all the pressures of the incoming administration, would probably have been compelled to follow suit.

It is conceded by some contemporary historians as well as by most modern scholars that this would have put a stop to secession. "No fact is clearer," wrote James Ford Rhodes, "than that the

Republicans in December defeated the Crittenden Compromise; few historic probabilities have better evidence to support them," he added, "than the one which asserts that the adoption of this measure would have prevented the secession of the cotton States, other than South Carolina, and the beginning of the Civil War in 1861." Even had Seward not been able to persuade two Republican colleagues on the committee to join him in support of Crittenden's proposals, it would not have been fatal to the plan. For, as we shall see, his influence in subsequent Senate deliberations would have been sufficient to order a national plebiscite on Crittenden's proposals that might well have stayed the bitter strife that followed their rejection.

The refusal of Republicans to accept division of the territories into slave and free-soil sections seems, even in light of the knowledge they possessed, as shortsighted and unstatesmanlike as was the conduct of southern extremists in urging secession because of the refusal. It had long been conceded by all knowing men, North as well as South, that slavery would never prosper there. Popular sovereignty, for all the Republican denunciation of it, actually was working to exclude slavery in the territories as effectively as congressional prohibition could. But Republicans had taken their position on the question long before, some of them decades before, at a time when the eventual triumph of the free-soil element had not yet been demonstrated as it had been everywhere by 1860. The party had been formed to prevent the spread of slavery into the territories at a time when that prospect seemed an imminent probability in Kansas. To concede now that the danger no longer existed for which they had organized would be an admission that popular sovereignty had already achieved the end for which they had waged their battle. In the absence of any program as a substitute, such an admission might result in dissolution of the party.

It needs to be emphasized, also, that the terms the South was willing to accept were actually a restriction of the lawful limits of slavery. For the Supreme Court had ruled in 1857, in the Dred Scott case, that Congress could put no restriction on slavery in any of the territories. Within two months the Republicans would demonstrate the hollowness of their own cries of alarm. Before the inauguration of Lincoln, the Republican-controlled Congress passed bills for territorial governments in Colorado, Nevada, and Dakota, containing no prohibition of slavery. Even such a stouthearted Republican as James G. Blaine commented in afteryears on this strange anomaly—

Republicans disregarding their very *raison d'être* with never a word of protest. Washburne, Thaddeus Stevens, Owen Lovejoy, Wade, Sumner—all of them were thundering at that very moment that Crittenden's proposal was a betrayal of the principles on which the country was founded, but none raised his voice against the omission of an antislavery provision in these bills. Daniel Sickles in the House called attention to the omission. He asked that the Colorado bill be read again before a vote was taken, not believing he properly understood it. When it was read, he pointed out that the Wilmot principle of the Republicans had been abandoned. No Republican offered an explanation.

Even Seward admitted, after passage of these bills, that the territorial question was settled and that it had "ceased to be a practical question." Douglas, too, though not vindictively, could not refrain from pointing out to his Republican colleagues that they had abandoned in these bills the position of their President-elect, who claimed to have voted for the Wilmot Proviso forty-two times in his one congressional term. "The whole doctrine for which the Republican party contended as to the Territories is abandoned," said Douglas. "Non-interference is substituted in its place." He rightly maintained that this was the very principle enunciated in his Kansas-Nebraska bill, and Blaine conceded that this was so. Douglas called the territorial bills the "apotheosis of Popular Sovereignty."

In the light of all this, the refusal of the five Republican senators on the Committee of Thirteen to concede the heart of Crittenden's propositions calls for closer scrutiny. Three of them were radicals, Wade, Grimes, and Doolittle, the latter a less vindictive one than the other two. But Seward and Collamer were not. As we have seen, Seward's position, and in turn Collamer's also, was determined by Lincoln, and it now becomes necessary to try to analyze Lincoln's reasons for assuming such an inflexible position.

The stature that Lincoln would gain in the ensuing four years has created a legend about him that all but obscures the fact that at the time of his election, and for some months thereafter, he was a plain country lawyer with a narrowly limited background. He would soon prove that he had great undeveloped capacities for leadership and for sensing the feelings of the great masses of the people. In the winter of 1860-1861, however, he was being led by, rather than leading, his party. He was not regarded by most of his contemporaries as more than what he seemed to be. Orville Browning, perhaps his closest friend, never regarded him as a great man, and thought Edward Bates much abler. Jeremiah Black, Buchanan's stout Secretary of State, thought him "very small potatoes and few in a hill." Charles Francis Adams thought that Lincoln, by refusing to agree to Seward's desire for compromise, was "ruining everything" and was making Seward's position unbearable. Seward, however, acceded for the time to his chief's strong sentiments regarding the territories, hoping until the very last moment that in the end he would be able to control the man who had been chosen over him and bring the ship of state safely to shore.

In the ominous public silence that Lincoln maintained from his nomination until his inaugural, he revealed somewhat his failure to understand the temper of the southern people. He apparently thought that the average southerner could distinguish between Lincoln's own philosophy on the slavery question and that of abolitionists like William Lloyd Garrison. When asked to publicize his views, he refused, repeatedly. He also seemed to think that secession was largely talk on the part of a few hotheads, and would be easily put down by an overwhelming Unionist sentiment in the South. The Upper South he believed so steadfast that there was patently no danger of secession there. If there were, the border states would smother the sentiment. Meantime, he would hold his counsel until March 4, and then in a conciliatory message, he would give such assurances that all fear of him and his party would dissipate. Only twice between his election and his inaugural did he permit himself the luxury of a public statement on the troubled condition of the country, both times by proxy. On the first of these occasions he wrote an insertion for a speech Trumbull delivered in Springfield, expressing pleasure over the military preparations that were underway in southern states. These would offer, he said, means for Unionists there more easily to suppress secession.

It was on December 20 that Weed had made his vain attempt to persuade Lincoln to recede on the territorial question, and on that very day South Carolina passed her ordinance of secession. When news of it reached Lincoln, he dismissed it as "loud threats and much muttering." A week later Duff Green arrived in Springfield as Buchanan's envoy, on a mission similar to Weed's. Green carried a copy of Crittenden's resolutions, and he and Lincoln discussed them for several hours. According to Green, Lincoln acknowledged that adoption of the Missouri line would calm southerners for a time, but soon they would renew the agitation by attempts to annex Mexico. Lincoln gave Green to understand that although he and his party were committed to resisting the expansion of slavery into the territories, he would both acquiesce in and "give full force and effect" to any decision by the people to adopt Crittenden's proposal as an amendment to the Constitution. He promised to write Green a letter the next day referring Crittenden's proposals "to the action of the people in the several states." Lincoln did write a letter addressed to Green, but he sent it to Trumbull in Washington to deliver to Green, if Trumbull and "our discreet friends" thought it would do no harm.

Apparently Trumbull and the friends did not approve of the letter, for they never delivered it to Green. Green thereupon gave a statement to the New York *Herald*, repeating what he understood Lincoln's position to be. The publication of this created consternation among radical Republicans in Washington, and Kellogg was dispatched to Springfield to confer with the President-elect. Then, on January 28, Kellogg published in the *Herald* a qualified retraction of Green's report. Kellogg was authorized to say that Lincoln would "suffer death" rather than enter into a bargain that would have the appearance of "buying the privilege of taking possession" of the government. This was the second and last of Lincoln's statements prior to his inaugural.

Lincoln had other visitors in Springfield. An unidentified Kentuckian, possibly Robert J. Breckinridge, went there in early December to suggest that Lincoln place three southern Unionists in his cabinet. Lincoln amazed his visitor by replying that he would appoint neither an "enemy" nor anyone who had voted against him. The Kentuckian argued for two hours, with Lincoln silent for the most part. At the end he thanked his visitor "for your counsel," but the latter was unhappy. His report of the interview caused Kentucky Unionist George Robertson to fear that if Lincoln's position should become known, southern fears of a "subterranean design to wage an exterminating crusade" against their section would be confirmed, and they would speedily secede.

Orville Browning, too, visited Lincoln at this time and found him firmer on the territorial question than he expected. According to Browning, Lincoln thought "no concession by the free states short of a surrender of everything worth preserving, and contending for would satisfy the South, and that Crittenden's proposed amendment . . . ought not to be made." Herndon, too, although frequently an unreliable witness, stated that Lincoln that winter said he "apprehended no such grave danger to the Union as the mass of people supposed would result from the Southern threats," and that he "could not in his heart believe that the South designed the overthrow of the government." Another Lincoln intimate, Ward Lamon, said Lincoln hoped for a peaceful reconstruction "even after the formation of the Southern Confederacy." Lincoln himself, in his journey east to his inaugural, demonstrated in speech after speech his belief that the secession movement was artificial and of little consequence.

Testimony of other contemporaries supports the belief that Lincoln was hopelessly confused and misinformed about political conditions in the South at this time. Horace Greeley wrote a few years later: "Mr. Lincoln entered Washington the victim of a grave delusion.... [H]e fully believed that there would be no civil war—no serious effort to consummate the Union.... [H]e did not cherish a doubt that his Inaugural Address ... would, when read throughout the South, dissolve the Confederacy as frost is dissipated by a vernal sun." No less convincing are the words of Charles Francis Adams, Jr. "As to the tremendous crisis which then confronted the country and himself individually,—the catastrophe immediately impending—if at that time Mr. Lincoln realized the situation he certainly ... gave no indication of the fact." Almost all recent scholarship agrees with these conclusions.

Believing that secession was only gasconade, Lincoln saw no purpose in stirring up the radicals in his own party by making unnecessary concessions. Many of these radicals, like Lincoln, thought secession a bluff. But many influential Republicans who thought it might result in war were unconcerned if it should. Herndon, returning from a tour of central Illinois, reported that the sentiment everywhere was for a firm stand on the platform regardless of consequences, and Trumbull's correspondence confirms this. It was "the very life blood—the corner stone of the party," wrote one constituent. If the party should surrender on the territorial question, "We are gone hook & line." Another wrote that surrender of the principle of the Chicago platform "would be the annihilation of the party." To yield one new guaranty to the South, wrote another Republican, would "destroy the Republican party."

Equally unconcerned as to consequences was Senator Zachariah Chandler of Michigan. "Without a little blood-letting," he wrote

Governor Austin Blair, "this Union will not . . . be worth a rush." And Governor Oliver Morton of Indiana, in a November speech urging coercion of South Carolina, said, "If it was worth a bloody struggle to establish this Nation, it is worth one to preserve it." These were powerful men in Republican circles, and Lincoln was not entirely impervious to their influence.

Lincoln expressed the fear to Duff Green that restoration of the Missouri line would lead to southern demands for territorial acquisition to the South, in Mexico, in the Caribbean, and in Central America. Crittenden's original proposal implied that any future acquisitions either south or north would be subject to terms of the division, and he subsequently accepted an amendment by Powell that made this explicit. Lincoln's fears on this score were not altogether imaginary. For years southern expansionists had dreamed of annexing additional territory in Mexico, as well as the island of Cuba. Filibustering expeditions in the past decade had not been uncommon occurrences, and just the year before, as we have seen, southern members of Congress had backed a bill to put $30,000,000 into Buchanan's hands to negotiate the acquisition of Cuba.

But sober reflection should have given Lincoln some reassurance on this point. Filibustering had been put down by both Whig and Democratic administrations; and if Cuban or Mexican territory could not be acquired under Pierce or Buchanan, there was little likelihood that it could be under a Republican President. Besides, as we shall see, Lincoln and the Republicans would not recede from their position even when Crittenden offered to add to his proposals a provision making future acquisitions of territory impossible without the express approval of northern members of Congress.

Thus it was that Crittenden's proposals were put to death in the Senate Committee of Thirteen in late December. Directly, their failure was due to the opposition of the five Republican members of the committee. Indirectly, the responsibility for their rejection was Lincoln's, who exerted from Springfield the vast influence that was his as President-elect.

(from John J. Crittenden:
The Struggle for the Union, *pp. 374-76, 382-89)*

WITHOUT DUE PROCESS

Although most Kentuckians probably breathed a sigh of relief as neutrality was replaced by unqualified commitment to the Union by the legitimate state government, many were soon to look back on the summer of neutrality as a period of comparative peace and happiness. For the strategic importance of the state made it imperative that the Federals hold it at all costs. To insure this they kept large numbers of Northern troops in the state. The behavior of some of the troops and their subordinate officers caused many Kentuckians to feel that they were aliens living in conquered territory.

Wholesale arrests were made without due process by overzealous marshals. Persons, some of them leading citizens and one of them a former governor, were seized on the barest suspicion and on the flimsiest of charges. Thousands were imprisoned in the state without indictment or trial and hundreds were rushed out of the state to northern prisons. Many women were imprisoned because they had a husband, a son, a father, or a brother in Confederate service. Test oaths were required of teachers and clergymen. All court officials including jurors were required to take a special oath, and courts suspected of disloyalty were shut down. Loyalty oaths were required of all suspects and death fixed as punishment for violation. Elections were interfered with by the military. Voters were intimidated and names of Peace Democrats were peremptorily removed from ballots. Runaway slaves were harbored by military officers; and raids were made on plantations and slaves carried off for military work. Commercial restrictions were such that Kentucky was treated as if it were part of the Confederacy. All trade south of Louisville required a permit which only the staunchest of Union men could get. Newspapers that could not be trusted could not buy news print. Because the region west of the Tennessee River was notoriously sympathetic to the Confederacy it was subjected to unusually harsh military rule. Heavy taxes were imposed by military fiat, property was confiscated and an uncertain number of civilian executions—some estimations as high as forty—took place.

The harsh military occupation did not revive the secessionist movement, however. Most Kentuckians distinguished between the government and the Lincoln administration and remained steadfast in their loyalty to the Union. Kentucky continued to give stout support to the war effort. She furnished about 75,000 men of the 90,000 requested of her. Considering the fact that probably 22,000 to 25,000 men of military age left the state for Confederate service, this was not a discreditable record.

(unpublished manuscript written in 1960 in anticipation of the Civil War centennial)

THE KENTUCKY SOLDIER IN THE CIVIL WAR

The Union majority in the Legislature took control of the State Guard from the secessionist-minded governor, Beriah Magoffin, and placed it under a newly created Military Board. As a further precaution they also created a rival military force, the Home Guard, made up of Unionists. Through the summer of 1861, as the Union Party in the state demonstrated its superiority, thousands of Confederate sympathizers slipped away to Tennessee and Virginia to fight for the Southern cause. Perhaps 10,000 of these were members of the State Guard, some of whom decamped as organized units.

Families were divided, frequently the father going one way and his son another, and scarcely a family but contributed sons to both camps. Families, churches, friendships, seemed to have little influence in determining the way men went. James Speed wrote Joseph Holt in October, 1861, that "so many of our giddy young men have gone into the Southern army, that almost every man who goes into our army, knows that he has to fight a neighbor, a relative, a brother, a son or father." Two brothers in the Fourth Kentucky Union infantry regiment at Missionary Ridge fought against two of their brothers in the Fourth Kentucky Confederate regiment which faced them there. . . .

About 11,000 Kentuckians in the Union army were Negroes, and their recruitment was the source of much discontent among the people who generally thought Negroes were inferior people not to be dignified with military duty. For a time, bowing to Kentuckians' protests, Lincoln delayed ordering Negro enrollments in the state.

But as white Kentuckians failed to make Kentucky's quota in April, 1864, General Burbridge ordered the enlistment of Negroes, both slave and free, with limited compensation to loyal masters.

This order created much discontent which extended over into the army. "Their is a great stir in camp about the negro question or Lincoln proclimation," wrote one soldier. "I am not in favor of fiting for negro freedom I did not start out on that platform. I hope he will modify Or drop the negro business give me the Unions as it was that suites me." Colonel Frank Wolford, a fearless cavalry leader from Casey County, in a speech in Lexington, denounced Lincoln as a tyrant and usurper, and for his pains was dismissed from the army. . . .

Despite embarrassments and difficulties by the beginning of 1865 the state's quota of troops had been met. At that time the state adjutant general reported that out of a total enrollment of 133,500 males between eighteen and forty-five, Kentucky had furnished more than 76,000 soldiers, while another 7,000 were enlisted but not mustered in, and 10,000 more were engaged as Home Guards. This was approximately ten per cent of the state's entire population. Add to this number 25,000 men in Confederate service and Kentucky's per capita contribution to the man power of the war was probably as great as that of any state. Nathaniel Shaler, Harvard anthropologist and historian, said that "No other State in the Union gave proportionately so much or so freely . . . to the cause of the Union."

Were Kentuckians typical of troops recruited from other states? Very likely they were, although from measurements carefully made and preserved by the United States Sanitary Commission, the Union medical corps, Kentuckians were better physical specimens than Union troops from any other state. Average height of the Kentucky soldier was 5 feet 8½ inches which was a half inch taller than his counterpart in any other state, and an inch taller than the average New Englander. The average Kentuckian weighed 149.85 pounds, four and a half pounds more than the typical soldier of any other state, and a full ten pounds heavier than the average New Englander.

More than 10,000 Kentuckians died in the War from battle wounds, and probably another 20,000 from disease during the War. Add to this the tens of thousands of maimed and diseased who did not die, and it is not unlikely that half of the Kentuckians who attained maturity in the decade of the 1850's and 1860's were either swept away or rendered unserviceable to the commonwealth by the war.

(from the Courier-Journal *Civil War Centennial Issue, magazine [November 20, 1960], p. 46)*

THE ORPHAN BRIGADE

One of the most celebrated bands of fighting men who participated in the Civil War was the First Kentucky or Orphan Brigade. The origin of its name is uncertain, [but] ... certain it is that during almost its entire existence the Brigade was "orphaned" from home. After its retreat from Bowling Green in February, 1862, its members never set foot on their native soil again until after their surrender.

It is doubtful if any other brigade in the Confederate Army saw such continuous and far-flung service as did the Orphans. Starting out from Bowling Green in the autumn in 1862 they fought in every major engagement in the West from Shiloh to Atlanta. During the intervening years they had marched, fought, and bled from one end of Tennessee to the other, through the burning hot sands of Mississippi and Louisiana, over the rough foothills and mountains of north Alabama and Georgia to the sea, and in the dying months of the war through the swamps of the Carolinas.

This closing chapter of the war in the West is a story of blind, unreasoning, almost superhuman courage and fortitude on the part of the men who fought on for what had for some time been a hopeless cause. Yet they seemed until the very end unable to grasp the meaning of defeat. The surprise and shock with which the Orphans received news of the surrender was indeed pathetic. They were sure, even on the last day, that right was on their side and that, somehow, in some way, right would triumph. The surrender was, one of them wrote, "the darkest day of our lives."

The saga of the Orphan Brigade reveals that it was no ordinary body of men, even in such a worthy company as the Army of

Tennessee. The men of the Orphan Brigade were volunteers in the purest meaning of that term. In the beginning all Confederate, as all Union soldiers, were volunteers. But as the early romantic impressions of war and early enthusiasm of patriotism waned conscription became necessary. The Confederate states began conscripting early in 1862, and from that time on as attrition depleted the ranks of the old volunteer units, they were refilled with the fruits of the Conscription Act. . . .

But the Orphans had all joined up in the first year of the war. Kentucky at the time had declared her neutrality, and sentiment in the state was pro-Union, soon to become overwhelmingly so. There was, therefore, little pressure on them, even of sentiment, impelling them to enlist. Indeed, they went in many cases in opposition to the wishes of their families and friends and the opinion of their community. Whether they went from constitutional conviction or from emotional attachment to a cause matters little; they were determined and devoted men, the circumstances of whose enlistment were quite different from those whose states had seceded. Furthermore, the Confederacy was without power to enforce the draft in Kentucky. Consequently, as battle and disease took their toll in the Brigade, the vacant places were not filled with unwilling draftees; they were simply left vacant, and the survivors closed ranks and carried on. The regiments comprising the Brigade at their organization had counted approximately 5,000 men. When they left Dalton in May, 1864, this number had dwindled to 1,420. At the time of the surrender there were fewer than three hundred.

Despite this heavy attrition the enthusiasm and discipline of the Orphans never waned. General Wheeler, under whom they served in the Savannah campaign, wrote, "No men in the Confederate States have marched more, fought more, suffered more, or had so little opportunities for discipline; yet they are today as orderly and as well disciplined as any cavalry in the Confederate service. . . . I must particularly commend my Kentucky troops, who . . . I brought from the Coosa River to Savannah without a single desertion."

(from the Courier-Journal *Civil War Centennial Issue, magazine [November 20, 1960], p. 95)*

HOW DID THE PEOPLE KEEP BODY
AND SOUL TOGETHER

In the four years from 1861 to 1865 the American nation struggled through the supreme crisis of its existence. Southern delusions that states could step peaceably out of the Federal Union as an exercise of a right; that a new nation of 5,500,000 whites and 3,500,000 slaves spread over a third of the land area of the Union could not be conquered and subjugated by an emotionally and politically divided North; that unlimited agricultural resources and industrial supplies from a friendly Europe would provide all necessary prerequisites to defense, were swept away in the storm of places like Shiloh and Gettysburg and Atlanta. Northern delusions that the whole business would be settled in ninety days were shattered by the pitiful dead of a hundred fields.

In the endless literature of that celebrated war the fortitude and valor of the Confederate soldier has become part of the national heritage—and deservedly so if records, official and unofficial, are to be credited. However, no more than a few hundred thousand Confederates were ever in service at any one time—a small fraction of the total population of the South. What of the rest of the people? Neglected in song and story, the civilian and the life he led must be studied if we would understand the Confederacy.

Life behind the lines, though drastically affected by the war, went on its inevitable way. Whether the armies won victories or suffered defeats, the people at home had to live; and living they knew joy and hope, suffered pain and despair, sought consolation in religion or amusement, sang paeans to their leaders when things went well and railed against them when things went bad.

But what was life like in the Confederacy? Did this great tragic experience produce poets who wrote in heroic verse of their supreme adventure? If not, were Southern critics aware of the new nation's literary limitations? Was there hope for creation of a national literature? What did religious leaders have to say about slavery, and what stand did they take on secession? What of education? Were Southerners content with the less than adequate schools of their region, or did they hope to do something about them? What of graphic arts, of agriculture, of manufacturing?

How did the people keep body and soul together when flour sold for $300 a barrel and bacon for $10 a pound? How did they clothe themselves when overcoats sold for $1,000 and boots for $250 a pair? How deep did patriotism run? Were there many who took advantage of neighbor and country by demanding exorbitant prices for necessities, or did most dedicate themselves to victory? Northern speculators connived, with their government's approval, to purchase cotton at handsome prices. Were Southerners seduced into this illegal trade?

What of politics? Was it a mistake to choose Jefferson Davis to lead the new government? Would things have gone better under an abler man, such as perhaps, Robert Toombs or Howell Cobb? Or was independence an unattainable dream and Davis the best available man, as Robert E. Lee seemed to think he was? Alexander Stephens may have contributed to the final collapse by his public denunciation of administration policy and his personal attacks on Davis; was it a mistake, in the name of unity, to elect a reluctant secessionist like Stephens to office? Would it have been better to let men who had led the revolution head the new government? Davis surrounded himself with some counselors who had little popular support, or were considered mediocrities who simply carried out instructions from their chief; was he wise in loyally sustaining these officials despite the opposition they provoked? Did Judah P. Benjamin, for all his intellectual powers, strengthen or weaken the administration? Was conscription, under the circumstances, the best way to raise an army, or was Joseph E. Brown right in denouncing it as unnecessary and unconstitutional? Did Davis injure the cause by interfering with his generals, or would it have been better, as one of his critics thought, if "some honest planter" who did not think of himself as a military genius had headed the government? Was it stubbornness that induced Davis to support Braxton Bragg after he had lost the confidence of rank and file? Many charged that favoritism influenced choice of army officers and civil officials as well. Was it bad judgment or pettiness or both that caused Davis to remove Joseph E. Johnston as commander of the Army of Tennessee before Atlanta in July 1864?

Hindsight suggests that the government was unwise in its cotton policy—that in order to build up foreign credit it should have exported cotton before the blockade became effective. But would foreign credit have been of great value in 1863 and later when the Union navy was cutting imports to a fraction of the need? The Confederate Congress was roundly denounced for causing inflation by failure to tax and by deciding to fight the war on borrowed money; was the Congress at fault, or was the constitutional restriction on taxation, together with popular opposition to taxes, the real cause?

The all-pervading influence during the years of the Confederacy was, of course, the war itself. It crowded into all facets of the day-by-day life of the citizen. It made its way to his table and devoured the food he had husbanded for his wife and children; it sat beside his hearth and consumed the warmth that should have driven the chill from his house; it reached its hand into his pocket and took the coin that would have purchased necessities; it accompanied him into the market place and gathered up the goods that would have been abundant; it went with him to church where he prayed for victory or heard sermons condemning the invaders; it sat beside him in the theater; it pushed into his sick chamber and snatched away his medicines; and at night it lay down beside him in his bed, wrapped itself in his blanket, and left him only a few hours of cold and comfortless sleep.

The Confederacy did not use all its resources, either human or material, in fighting the war, but it probably came as close to doing so as any nation since Carthage. To have conducted the war properly, the government would have had to centralize control of the economy. Conscription, detailing, licensing, and price-fixing were attempts at this, but they met such opposition that their effect was largely nullified. Could the administration, public opinion being what it was, have gone further than it did toward centralization? In other words, was State rights compatible with the facts of nineteenth-century life?

Finally, there is the matter of foreign policy. From the outset, influential people in England and France favored recognition of the Confederacy, and even intervention. Aid from abroad might have insured the Confederacy's independence, and no efforts should have been spared by the Davis government to obtain it. One factor working against recognition was the seeming inability of the South to launch a successful military offensive. A single military victory on Northern soil might well have brought diplomatic dividends out of all proportion to sacrifices such a campaign would entail. Only a few more divisions made available to Lee in the summer of 1862 might have made the abortive Maryland campaign a brilliant success. Could not these divisions have been drawn from North Carolina or Tennessee? What doomed the Confederacy to the use of three-quarter measures at such a time?

Another deterrent to foreign recognition of the Confederacy was its "peculiar institution." Of course, slavery was the underlying cause of secession, and perhaps the idea of emancipation was unthinkable to the South in the early years of the war. Yet, a few months before the end, the Confederate government offered Britain emancipation in return for recognition. Although the time had long passed when there was any prospect of British recognition, might not the offer two years earlier have borne fruit?

(from The Confederacy, *pp. 13-17)*

THE GATES TO A FUTURE

Thus far we have considered only the negative influence of the Civil War on Southern society. War is a destructive agency, and it is not orthodox to associate it with progressive or constructive forces. Yet if freedom and democracy and education are positive influences—and most Americans take it for granted that they are—then the Civil War was not wholly without benign influence on Southern society as a whole, even though the cost of improvement was unnecessarily high. For the war was the beginning of the end to an archaic order which was a retarding influence on mid-nineteenth century patterns of society.

The Negro had been given, for a time under Reconstruction, the right to vote. Unprepared as he was for this privilege, the use he made of it was not inspiring. Reconstruction scandals were to become legendary wherever Southern politics were discussed. But it is doubtful if voting practices in the South at the time were more corrupt than they were in New York and Philadelphia and St. Louis. And "Boss" Tweed, W. W. Belknap, John McDonald, Oakes Ames, and other swindlers in the North could learn little, if anything, from Southern politicians. The fact was, however, that the Negro was for the first time making use of the ballot. He might use it poorly. But it was a beginning for him in the practice of democracy, and he would fight in years to come to improve this opportunity.

But political activity was only one gleam in the Negro's eye. Even before the war ended Southern schools were started by the Freedman's Bureau and by northern philanthropists, principally for the benefit of Negro children. Soon there came public schools for all the children in the Southern states, both white and Negro. They were woefully inadequate. For decades to come they would operate only a few months each year, and their teachers often were only a few years academically in advance of their backward scholars. But poor as these schools were, they were the only schools masses of the South, had ever known. These people were at least, learning to read and to write, and this was far more intellectual activity than they had known under the old regime.

The conclusion seems obvious, that despite the tragedy and desolation brought on by the war, for great numbers of depressed people in the South, Negroes and yeoman whites, too, the war could not be measured in negative terms only. To them it opened the gates to a future, that bleak and forbidding as it seems to us in retrospect, was progress over that they had ever known before.

(from "The Defeated," a paper read before the Mississippi Valley Historical Association, Louisville, April 29, 1960)

CIVIL RIGHTS

Violence   139
The Negro   139
The Southern Penal System   143
Franchise and Apportionment   144
Southern Labor   146
Segregation and Black Handicaps   149
Exit Jim Crow   153

VIOLENCE

The ante-bellum South had been a land where individuals settled their difficulties by personal encounter, whether by the code, or by less genteel standards. The Civil War rather accentuated this characteristic. Postwar Southerners delighted in arming themselves with the pistol and the knife, and crimes of violence filled the news columns. Stories of "murder, rape, robbery, arson, assault and battery, thievery, and malfeasance in office were as commonplace as notices of camp meetings and barbecues." In less than a twenty year period around the turn of the century there were more than 2500 "unofficial executions" in the South, or three times as many as occurred in the rest of the country during the same period. Men killed one another sometimes because of imagined wrongs to themselves or to their women, or even to their dogs. The chief sufferer from these acts of uninhibited violence was, again, the Negro. By 1870 lynching had become a pattern in the Southern states, and in the years between 1888 and 1903 there were more than two hundred lynchings of Negroes in Georgia alone.

(from "The Defeated," a paper read before the Mississippi Valley Historical Association, Louisville, April 29, 1960)

THE NEGRO

Emancipation of the Negro had made him no longer a marketable chattel subject to sale, and to this extent it had freed him from the bonds of involuntary servitude. This was, of course, a giant stride forward for the Negro. But for the better part of a century thereafter his progress seemed interminably slow; indeed, at times he seemed to retrogress. For gains won in the aftermath of the Civil War during radical reconstruction were soon lost, and he slid backward into a despised state of neglect and isolation which in some features seemed more degrading even than slavery. Under slavery he had at least been a valuable chattel. . . .

With the abandonment of the Negro by his northern protectors after 1877, he was again returned to the mercy of native whites. But there would be a difference now. Under slavery the vast majority of non-slaveowning whites had been largely isolated from the Negro, and there had been only a labor issue between the white man and his slave. Under the new order there would be created a race issue. In a sense and to a degree, all whites had been aristocrats under slavery because they were free. After redemption, white men who had seen Negroes occupy superior positions to their own during radical reconstruction were resolved that it should not happen again. Accordingly, they set about creating a caste system based, not on law as was slavery, but on biological inferiority. In this new order the Negro would be the bottom layer, regardless of wealth or personal merit; even lower than he had been in slavery, for then he had looked down upon the poor white. And it became the principal aim of the new southern society to see that the Negro did not rise above this lowly position.

Under slavery there had been no occasion for social segregation. The Negro's status was so clearly inferior that artificial barriers were unnecessary. There was no need for segregation laws in education; for public schools, except in cities, were almost nonexistent even for white children, and there was no inclination to educate the Negro even if laws had permitted. Nor was there felt to be a need to enforce segregation in other areas. Slaves and masters traveled on the same coaches, ate at the same restaurants, occasionally attended the same theaters. Even after the end of the war, compulsory public segregation was not instituted at once. In Columbia, South Carolina, the freedman was admitted to all public assemblies; in Charleston he was barred from indoor theaters, but he could attend circuses, camp meetings, and "shows under canvas." There were even a few cases of intermarriage between the races, more often between white men and Negro women, although interracial marriages were frowned upon.

In a reaction to what southern whites regarded as the excesses of radical reconstruction, local ordinances in redeemed states began to require racial segregation in public accommodations. Consequently, just before the end of reconstruction, in 1875, Congress passed the Civil Rights Act. This act provided that all persons, regardless of race, were entitled to full and equal enjoyment of accommodations in public conveyances on land or water, at inns, theaters, and other places of public amusement. That the idea of compulsory segregation was still not deeply engrained is witnessed by the fact that the Congressional law was supported by legislation passed in some states with little opposition. As late as 1885 Negroes rode freely in first-class railway coaches in South Carolina and Virginia. They served on juries, attended political conventions as delegates, and their dead were even laid away in common burial grounds. In 1891, the Tillman-controlled South Carolina legislature defeated a Jim Crow railway bill. At the time the Charleston *News and Courier* observed that it was "a great deal pleasanter to travel with respectable and well behaved colored people than with unmannerly and ruffianly white people."

But relations between the races were already deteriorating. In 1883 the Supreme Court had ruled that while states were forbidden to abridge the privileges of citizens, private corporations might do so without violating the Civil Rights Act. Thereafter, as Negroes began moving into industrial towns where they competed with white workers for jobs, the demand for segregation laws grew, and between 1887 and 1891, nine southern states had provided for Jim Crow railway cars. By the turn of the century all southern states had done so. When these laws were tested, the Supreme Court ruled in the case of *Plessy v. Ferguson* (1896) that segregation was not in itself discrimination so long as the separate accommodations were equally good or bad for both races.

Soon there followed more comprehensive laws: segregation on street cars, in waiting rooms, dining cars, restaurants, and in sleeping accommodations. From these laws the states moved rapidly to segregation in courts, prisons, schools, factories, libraries, parks, playgrounds, theaters, hotels, hospitals, barber shops, cemeteries, and residential districts—anything that might suggest social equality. By the second decade of the twentieth century members of the two races were becoming isolated from one another in all phases of society save that which clearly identified the Negro as an inferior. It was a paradox that passage of these laws coincided with the democratic revolution in the South when the Farmers' Alliance was capturing control of legislatures and while progressive leaders like Vardaman, Aycock, and Hoke Smith were overthrowing regimes of the conservative redeemers.

Segregation was maintained throughout the period on the theory laid down in *Plessy v. Ferguson:* that the separate accommodations must be equal. Almost invariably, however, Negro accommodations were inferior and markedly so. In districts where Negroes did not vote the inequality extended beyond accommodations in public institutions: streets in Negro sections of cities went unpaved, public utility service was more primitive, police and judicial systems were organized to prevent equal protection for Negroes. Negroes were never placed equitably on public payrolls, and higher paid jobs were completely closed to them. These conditions prevailed for more than half a century; indeed, nothing was done to improve them until the New Deal of the 1930's. Then the federal government would make gallant efforts to eliminate the worst of the discriminations, but even then, as we have seen, it was more difficult for Negroes to get on relief rolls than whites in similar circumstances, and when they did get on their grants were smaller. A generation after the New Deal, in 1965, the Secretary of Agriculture admitted that there was still discrimination against Negro farmers in the South in his department's programs. The federal Civil Rights Commission, at the same time, charged that "there are two distinct Southern agricultural economies—one white and the other Negro," and as a result, Negroes were relegated to a separate, inferior, and outdated agricultural economy.

Discrimination was justified by whites on the ground that Negroes paid little taxes and thus received more benefits from government than they were entitled to, but never was this excuse thought to apply to the poor white who also paid little taxes. Nor was the fact that a few wealthy Negroes paid high taxes thought reason enough to secure them greater public benefits than poor Negroes. The determination to "keep the Negro in his place" varied in intensity among upper and lower class whites. The upper classes had no fear that the Negro would challenge their social position or compete with them economically. The lower classes, however, were threatened by the freedman's economic competition and were determined to set up and maintain a social distinction. Political pressure from lower-class whites swung upper-class whites to support of their program.

(from The South since Appomattox, *pp. 305-8)*

THE SOUTHERN PENAL SYSTEM

A profound but seldom mentioned result of the Civil War was the impact it had on the Southern penal system. Slavery was a total system which had embraced all aspects of Negro existence. All punishment, except for a relatively few capital crimes, had been meted out upon the plantation, and freedom brought an end to this as to other elements of the peculiar institution. Accordingly, four million ignorant freedmen, with undeveloped social and moral codes, were suddenly thrust upon an impoverished society already overburdened with seemingly insoluble problems. As in the case of roads and schools, states lacked penitentiaries and needs must shift all correction responsibilities back to private hands. Penitentiary boards were authorized to lease convicts, the vast majority of whom were Negroes, to planters and railroad contractors. Compared to the treatment accorded these convicts slavery had been a mild and humane institution. Even where no personal affection had existed between master and slave, the slave's welfare had coincided with the master's interest. The death or incapacity of the slave resulted in considerable loss to the master. But under the convict-lease system no such conditions prevailed. The convict was not apt to appeal to his lessee's affections, and the absence of ownership discouraged the lessee's interest in his welfare. If the convict was sick or disabled, or if he should die, he was replaced by a healthy substitute. Under such circumstances economy would call for the greatest exaction of labor from the convict in return for the least expenditure for his welfare, and such seems to have been the practice.

Statistics for the years 1881-1885 showed an annual mortality rate of more than 11 percent for Mississippi convicts, and at some periods it ran as high as 17 percent, while rarely dropping below 10 percent. At the same time the rate was slightly above 1 percent in Iowa, Illinois, and Ohio. A grand jury investigation of the penitentiary hospital in Mississippi, found twenty-six inmates lately returned from farms and railroads, some with consumption, some with their backs cut in "great wales, scars, and blisters." Some had frostbitten hands and feet, and all had "the stamp of manhood almost blotted out of their faces." "They are lying there dying," said the jury report, "some of them on bare boards, so poor and emaciated that their bones almost come through their skin." Vermin crawled over their faces, and their bedding was in tatters and stiff with filth. The report concluded that the system "takes a poor creature's liberty and [turns] him over to one whose interest it is to coin his blood into money."

The system was not materially changed at the end of the century. On the contrary such huge profits were to be made from it, that the leasing of convicts on shares became one of the patronage prizes in Southern state elections on into the early decades of the twentieth century.

(from "The Defeated," a paper read before the Mississippi Valley Historical Association, Louisville, April 29, 1960)

FRANCHISE AND APPORTIONMENT

Another problem with which the [Mississippi] Constitutional Convention of 1890 had to deal was that of apportionment of the state legislature. . . . Apportionment was as bitterly debated in the convention as were the clauses restricting the franchise, for the black county delegates were as reluctant to give up their control as the white county delegates were eager to wrest it from them. Many proposals were made, but that of Senator [James Z.] George prevailed and was adopted by the convention. According to George, his plan was based on "voting population" rather than on total population. It purported to create a majority of white constituencies by increasing the number of representatives in the legislature by thirteen and allotting the increase to the white counties. In addition, several legislative districts were carved out of white sections of black counties. Another provision created an electoral system of choosing the governor, each county being allotted electoral votes corresponding to its number of representatives. The unit system was established, and the candidate who carried a county received the electoral vote of that county. To be elected, however, a candidate must receive both a majority of the popular vote and a majority of the electoral vote. In case no candidate should receive both, the election was to be decided by the House of Representatives, which was to choose between the two candidates receiving the highest popular vote. The professed object of this apportionment was the erection of "an impregnable barrier to any possible organization of the Negro majority, by extraneous force or internal faction for political dominance." . . .

In a remarkable speech before the convention, Montgomery, the only Negro in the body, defended both the franchise clauses and the apportionment. He estimated that the franchise provision would disqualify more than 123,000 Negroes, but he was willing to sacrifice them "upon the burning altar of liberty" for the easing of the tension between the races. He believed that the apportionment plan would return a majority of fourteen legislators from white constituencies, but he was willing, he said, to make this sacrifice in the interest of better government.

Senator George said that the proposed apportionment plan would erect an impregnable barrier to any threat of Negro dominance. He argued that the provision was necessary because the federal courts might declare the franchise restrictions unconstitutional, and because a national Republican administration might enforce Negro voting at elections. The opinion seems to have been unanimous that the apportionment would meet such a challenge and that, under it, white supremacy would be guaranteed even though all Negro men were permitted to vote. This was called by Mississippi's most prolific historian "the legal basis and bulwark of the design of white supremacy."

Such authority is impressive, but an examination of the census does not justify such confidence. The apportionment was said to be based upon the "voting population" instead of the total population. If this "voting population" was comprised of all male adults, the claim that it in fact would have given a majority of legislators to districts with white majorities is questionable.

On the contrary the census of 1890 shows that if all male adults in every legislative district in Mississippi had voted, and if they had divided on race lines, Negroes would have returned 69 representatives and whites 64. In 1900, according to census figures, such a hypothetical vote would have returned the same number of whites and Negroes as in 1890, and in 1910 there would have been 71 Negroes and 66 whites. Not until 1920 would shifts of population and creation of new counties have given the whites a majority of the legislators. In that year an election by all male adults on race lines would have returned 77 whites and 63 Negroes.

After 1890 there was, therefore, not only a gross inequality of legislative representation as compared to eligible white voting population, but also to the actual number of votes cast in the several counties. That delegates from the white counties should have failed to see this is almost unbelievable. There is no evidence that they protested against the apportionment clause on such grounds. The only protest came from delegates from the black counties. True, the new apportionment would slightly decrease the representation of the black counties. But it would not and did not wrest governmental control from the hands of the comparatively small number of whites in the black counties. Even when the state-wide primary was established a dozen years later the black counties remained in control of the legislature. The apportionment provision has never had to meet the test for which it was professedly designed. Negro disfranchisement, illegally effected before 1890 and legally since, has been so complete as to spare the apportionment provision the failure which it must have faced prior to 1920 had the Negro voted as freely as the white man and on race lines.

(from Revolt of the Rednecks, *pp. 78-80, 82-84)*

SOUTHERN LABOR

The products of southern manufacture were typically standardized, industrial goods. The producers were numerous and small, and not subject to industry-wide collective bargaining on the part of labor even if there had been a disposition on the part of southern workers toward unionism, which there was not, as we have already seen. In 1928 the four leading manufacturing industries of the region—textiles, furniture, steel, and lumber—were almost completely unorganized. The road of the labor organizer was a rocky one in southern communities, where the people were unfamiliar with unions and where the workers lived in mill towns that were citadels of paternalistic capitalism.

Despite this milieu of social conservatism, a wave of unrest, provoked by pay cuts or the stretch-out, swept the textile industry of the South in the spring of 1929. Strikes of a somewhat spontaneous nature erupted in eastern Tennessee and in the piedmont regions of the Carolinas. Organized labor was in difficulty throughout the country at the time, but these strikes were the signal for organizers from the United Textile Workers of the American Federation of Labor to enter the controversy in an effort to furnish leadership to the workers. At Marion, North Carolina, a strike occurred when management began laying off workers who had joined the UTW. When picket lines were set around the mills, management called on the governor for troops. These were sent and soon brought the strikers to accept a settlement. A month later when management, in violation of the settlement, again began discharging union members, the workers struck again. Tension mounted, and when sheriff's deputies used tear gas in breaking up a picket line, firing started. When the smoke cleared, not a deputy had been shot, but thirty-six strikers lay wounded, six of them mortally. The deputies who did the shooting were identified and indicted, but all were acquitted. Meanwhile, four strikers were tried for "rioting," convicted, and given jail sentences.

At Elizabethton, Tennessee, at about the same time, 5000 workers struck two German-owned rayon plants. Grievances were the same as elsewhere: long hours, low wages, and the stretch-out. Although rayon was a new textile industry, much more profitable than cotton or wool, wages paid were no higher than in the more depressed branches of the industry. In the department where the walk-out started, 550 girls were employed fifty-six hours a week at an average weekly wage of $8.96, or sixteen cents an hour. In another department, a man with wife and children earned $12 a week from which he paid monthly rent of $25 plus an additional $1.50 for water and $2.25 for light. Fuel and food had to be purchased independently, and there was no company store in Elizabethton to extend credit.

Within six days the strike had closed both plants completely. Court orders were obtained, enjoining strikers from picketing, and the governor of Tennessee sent eight hundred federally armed state militia to enforce the orders. Streets bristled with soldiers, and machine guns were installed on the roofs of buildings. As at Marion, a settlement was reached and later violated by the companies. When the workers walked out a second time, pickets were arrested and two of the leaders who had been sent in by the UTW were kidnapped and carried out of the state. Soon strikers' families were going hungry, for the AFL, which had discouraged the strike, gave little help to the strikers other than moral support. Morale crumbled, and after ten weeks a settlement was reached on company terms. No provision was made for union recognition, and 1000 union members were blacklisted.

The most serious disturbances of the period occurred at Gastonia, North Carolina, where the strikers were led by Fred Beal and George Pershing, organizers sent in by the National Textile Workers Union, a Communist-controlled rival of the UTW. Although the struck mills were owned by Rhode Island industrialists, community sentiment, through the media of press and pulpit, openly supported them and condemned the strikers. Regional patriotism, religion, loyalty to the Lost Cause, the idea of white supremacy, all joined with the native fear of the Red menace to brand the strikers as subversives. Civil liberties were violated as police authorities and strikebreakers united to harass the strikers and their leaders. Finally violence broke out when a mob of masked men destroyed the strike headquarters.

Liberal editors and educators, including President William Louis Poteat of Wake Forest College and President Harry Woodburn Chase of the University of North Carolina, protested against violation of the civil rights of the strikers, but the effect of their protest was lost when Gastonia Police Chief O. F. Aderholt was killed while attempting to break up a strikers' meeting. At almost the same time, a woman striker named Ella Mae Wiggins was killed when armed men fired from an automobile into the truck in which she was riding to a strikers' meeting. Fred Beal was not even present at the scene of Aderholt's killing, but he and six other strike leaders were indicted for "conspiracy to murder." No credible evidence was presented at the trial to substantiate the charges, but the defendants were convicted and sentenced to prison terms of from five to twenty years. The identity of the man who actually did kill Ella Mae Wiggins was clearly established, but he was acquitted.

The strike was doomed from the outset. Gastonia, like most southern communities, regarded the principle of unionism as a move against progress and against the inalienable right of an employer to fix the conditions of employment. Perhaps the greatest of the forces working against the strikers' success was the lack of unity that existed within the labor movement in the South. At Gastonia, the greatest textile-manufacturing center in the country, only a handful of mills were involved, and the workers of the fifty or more unaffected mills could not be persuaded to join in the movement, even though the same conditions against which the strikers were protesting prevailed in their own plants. Indeed, even in the mills that were struck, many workers refused to walk out and instead acted as strike breakers.

Although the strikes of 1929 failed, they marked a milestone for southern labor. The unions collapsed for the time, but out of the disturbances there grew a class consciousness among southern mill workers; and unionism, which had appeared unthinkable shortly before, just as the idea of a break in the political solidarity of the Democratic South had been unthinkable a year before, was now a reality. Henceforth southern labor unions would be more than a figment of the imagination.

Gastonia revealed, too, that a small segment of southern workers, like some in other sections, were prepared if necessary to follow Communist leadership for truly radical solutions to their problems. For it was apparent that the small core of strikers who remained militant after the first few weeks were well aware of the revolutionary aims of Beal and Pershing. Even to countless conservative southerners who were not members of the working class it was apparent, more so than in Populist or reconstruction times, that the South's economic life was controlled by financiers from Wall Street or industrialists from Pawtucket. Rightly or wrongly, they blamed the Yankee for the depressed condition of their own section. And as the depression deepened about them and more disorder threatened, many began to despair of recovery under the old order. Whatever chance there may have been of a real revolutionary movement developing, however, was forestalled by the coming of the New Deal.

(from The South since Appomattox, *pp. 232-35)*

SEGREGATION AND BLACK HANDICAPS

Whether in large cities or small towns, the urban Negro lived in segregated neighborhoods. The Civil Rights Act of 1866 gave the

Negroes the right to hold land just as whites, and in 1917 the Supreme Court nullified a Louisville, Kentucky, ordinance restricting Negroes to one section of the city. Thereafter, practical segregation was effected throughout the South as in much of the North through private restrictive covenants in deeds. These were upheld by the Supreme Court in 1926, but voided after 1948, when the Court reversed itself. Economic conditions, however, as well as social mores, generally proved sufficient to prevent southern Negroes from moving into upper-class white neighborhoods. As a result they generally crowded into tenements or into back alleys in one- or two-room shacks which rented exorbitantly for 15 or 20 percent of cash value. Often the neighborhoods had no sewers, or if they did the houses had no plumbing, and outdoor toilets served many families.

Under the American political system where public officials are so responsive to voters' sentiments, the disfranchised southern Negro was doubly disadvantaged by segregation in slum areas. Officials did not need to see that streets were paved or lighted, that there were adequate hospitals, schools, sewers, garbage disposal; for it was well known that people living in those neighborhoods did not vote in great numbers. On the other hand, where Negroes were permitted to vote as in the upper South in general and in some large cities in the deep South, neighborhoods were rewarded with improved streets, playgrounds, housing projects. Negroes in Atlanta defeated a bond issue until they were assured of adequate schools, and Negroes in Dallas in 1939 were given a high school and a graded school after they supported a bond issue there. These developments seemed to demonstrate the truth of the contention that all progress for the Negro in the South was dependent upon his securing political power.

But all southern Negroes did not fall into only the two classes of farm and urban labor. Just as segregation caused a breakdown of communication between the races, it created the necessity for the black man to design a social order of his own. He did this by copying the white man's: excluded from participation in the white world, the Negro built a duplicate. As segregation became established, the Negro soon developed social and economic classes and the institutions which accompanied them: churches, schools, banks, theaters, professions, and other services. In this society, the business and professional man occupied first place, just as he did in the white. Education and lightness of color also helped determine class. Negro professionals, although excluded from serving white clients, had almost a monopoly of the black. They were, therefore, in the paradoxical position of both suffering from segregation and benefiting from it.

But there were additional handicaps suffered by Negro professionals. Negro teachers, whether in the schools or in the colleges, taught only Negroes. Negro doctors could not as a rule practice in southern hospitals. They were denied opportunity for internships and residencies, clinical facilities, and membership in county and state medical societies. This tended to make all of them general practitioners. Since extension of public health service caused them to lose their patients, they were opposed to all "socialized medicine" schemes. Negro lawyers were few in number, comprising less than one-half of one percent of the bar in most rural southern states. Rarely did they appear in court to defend Negroes against white litigants, but confined their efforts to criminal practice and to disputes between Negroes.

Probably because of the great insecurity that surrounded his everyday life, the southern Negro moved but slowly toward a stable family life. Marriage among slaves was unknown to the law of the Old South, and sexual promiscuity was not only practiced by slaves but often encouraged by masters. Invading Union armies disrupted what meager family life did exist on the plantations, and the completely demoralized Negroes who wandered about the country in the wake of the armies became extremely dissolute. In reconstruction days, marriage was legalized and gradually accepted, although there continued for decades to be much cohabiting without benefit of clergy, particularly in the rural South, where conditions of society more nearly resembled those of slave times. Women were "heads of families" in more than a fifth of southern Negro households, while fewer than a twelfth of white households were without a husband and father. . . .

It is almost universally believed that Negroes have been more criminal than whites and statistics seem to bear out this belief. But statistics on crime, unreliable at best, are even less trustworthy in regard to Negroes. The FBI's annual report for 1964, for instance, disclosed that Negroes, who made up only 11 percent of the country's population, accounted for more than 28 percent of the crime. But Roy Wilkins of the NAACP pointed out quite properly the misleading implications of this announcement; for dragnet arrests for a crime committed by one or two people frequently resulted in the arrest of dozens of Negroes, most of whom were subsequently dismissed. But their names were in the record books as arrested on criminal charges, and in the public mind Negro arrests were equated with Negro crime.

Most Negro crime had to do with theft, generally petty theft, and mayhem. Much of the theft charged to southern Negroes may have been regarded by them as compensation for starvation wages and for exploitation by dishonest or unscrupulous landlords and storekeepers. Booker T. Washington, relating an incident when his mother stole a chicken from her master's coop and fed it to her hungry children, concluded that "No one could ever make me believe that my mother was guilty of thieving. She was simply a victim of the system of slavery." Rarely were Negroes guilty of "white collar" crimes, violation of anti-trust laws or income-tax evasion. They have also been relatively low in sex offenses.

In the years following emancipation the increase in Negro criminality was at least partly due to the convict-lease system. Another explanation for the unusually high incidence of Negro crime was the tendency on the part of southern police officials to assume the guilt of any Negro charged with crime or apprehended under conditions even faintly suspicious. This same inclination to assume the Negro's guilt existed among whites in general; thus, all-white juries, which prevailed everywhere in southern states, were easily persuaded by zealous prosecutors to convict Negroes on doubtful evidence that would not prevail against a white man. It is quite probable, therefore, that exclusion of Negroes from juries increased significantly Negro convictions for crime in the South.

Police brutality in exacting confessions, often from innocent Negroes, was also a factor in Negro crime statistics. The police, usually coming from classes that were socially insecure, with little education and training for their work, held the Negro in contempt and were notorious for the use of intimidation and violence on Negro suspects. When the violence resulted in the death of the suspect, the dead but unconvicted Negro became merely another criminal statistic. Of 479 Negroes killed by whites in the South in the dozen years between 1920 and 1932, 260, or over half, were killed by police. Nor were such victims always suspected felons. In 1945 a Negro named Hall was beaten to death by Sheriff Claude Screws of Baker County, Georgia. Hall was in jail for protesting the police beating of his aged father. In 1958 James Brazier was beaten to death while in jail at Dawson, Georgia, for participating in a civil rights protest; and a Negro was fatally shot by an Alabama state policeman in March 1965 while engaging in a peaceable demonstration protesting against disfranchisement. In 1954 alone the federal government prosecuted thirty-two police officials for brutality to Negroes, but without obtaining a conviction.

Of course, both police brutality and exclusion of Negroes from juries were manifestations of the total denial of political rights to the Negro in a society that was otherwise ultra-democratic in administering its system of justice. For judges, prosecutors, sheriffs, jailors, constables, and other administrative officials were elective and were thus responsive to the inclinations and prejudices of the voters. And since the Negro had no active part in selecting these officials, and since he had no part in the jury except to appear before it as a potential victim, the whole system—police, prosecutor, jailor, and jury—were arrayed against him. Thus, democracy itself, so long as the Negro had no active part in it, worked to his disadvantage in the quest for justice. It may well be, too, that part of the high Negro crime rate stems from the Negro's belief that he cannot obtain justice in the white man's courts and that he must exact it for himself.

(from The South since Appomattox, *pp. 315-16, 318-19)*

EXIT JIM CROW

At the time of the First World War, the Negro had been encouraged to believe that with victory would come a remarkable change in the American social order. The war was being waged to "make the world safe for democracy," and even the militant Du Bois had called on Negroes to close ranks until the Central Powers were defeated. But the Negro's hopes were not realized. By the time of World War II he was thoroughly disillusioned. In the North as well as in the South he was sullenly skeptical about the future. A Negro editor wrote of "this strange and curious picture, this spectacle of America at war to preserve the ideal of government by free men, yet clinging to the vestiges of the slave system." A young Negro draftee put it even more bluntly: "Just carve on my tombstone, 'Here lies a black man killed fighting a yellow man for the protection of a white man.' ". . .

A decade after the Second World War despite much progress, the Negro's lot everywhere, but especially in the South, was still far below that of the white. About twice as large a percentage of southern Negroes were farmers, they had about half the average income of whites, and more than three times as many were unskilled or service workers. In towns and cities more of them lived in inadequate housing, without running water or private toilets. Their death rate was one-third higher than that of whites. Not only did they attend segregated schools, they lived segregated lives. By 1955 their leaders had resolved that humility, patience, and forbearance had run their course and had failed utterly to improve the lot of their people. They now determined to lead the Negroes into a campaign of civil disobedience: of boycotts, sit-ins, demonstrations in the streets. . . .

The basic philosophy of the boycott was that of nonviolent resistance: refusal in a peaceable manner to co-operate with forces of segregation. Accompanying the nonviolent resistance was a determination among the Negro leaders to drill into their followers the conviction that they were, in their peaceable resistance, freeing the white man of a heavy burden. "We are not out to defeat or humiliate the white man," said [Martin Luther] King, "but to help him as well as ourselves." For, "the festering sore of segregation," was an indignity to all America, not just to Negroes. And victory would be, not victory alone for the Negro, but a victory "for justice, freedom, and democracy." To white segregationists he said: "We will match your capacity to inflict suffering with our capacity to endure suffering. . . ."

The disturbances of 1963-64 closely followed passage of a moderate Civil Rights bill in 1962. The original bill's stronger features had been watered down in committee, and the final bill was unable to insure liberties demanded by civil rights advocates. The disturbances thus became a prelude to the Civil Rights Act of July 1964. Not since reconstruction had a bill with such sweeping federal authority in this area been debated in Congress. . . .

As the period draws to a close, what are the prospects for the future? Indications are that despite the remarkable progress in recent years, the road to political, economic, and social justice for the Negro will still be a long and tortuous one. By individual achievement in almost every phase of American life the Negro has demonstrated the falsity of the charge that members of the race are incapable of intellectual or artistic excellence. Yet, the long period of discrimination he has suffered in all sections of the country and in all phases of life seems to have left the Negro with a feeling of inferiority which he cannot easily shed. Negro apathy toward political participation, even in the North; Negro lack of training for skilled jobs; inferior Negro education in most places—all these will retard economic progress for all but the few indomitables who will not be denied. Roy Wilkins expressed the fear that three hundred years of "first slavery and then segregation may have shredded the Negro's spiritual innards so badly that we will have to wait for another generation to do the intra-group, self-help work that must be done." At the same time and despite the injustice of it, the embarrassingly high Negro crime statistics will tend to hinder social acceptance for the race as a whole.

Much depends on the course now taken by moderate white southern politicians. Most southern Congressmen are too committed publicly to white supremacy to shift to an advocacy of Negro voting. But emancipation of the southern politician could be attained only when Negro voting strength there was such that the office-seeker would have to solicit Negro votes rather than demonstrate that he favored white supremacy more than his opponent. That day has not yet arrived. In the summer of 1965 it was estimated that fewer than half the eligible 5 million Negroes were registered, although the number had doubled in seven years. If equal percentages of both races were registered, Negro votes would be one-third of the white vote. If the Republican party should become a threat to the Democratic party, both parties would solicit the Negro vote. This would not only solve the Negro's political problem, it would revolutionize his social and economic position as well.

(*from* The South since Appomattox, *pp. 362-63, 369, 374-75*)

POLITICS

Old Court—New Court   159

Nostalgia for a Myth   172

Demagoguery and Reform   173

Demagoguery Evaluated   173

The Great Crusade and After   176

On the International Crisis   180

OLD COURT—NEW COURT

Henry Clay, to whose leadership Crittenden was to give unquestioning loyalty for more than thirty years and to whose fortunes Crittenden's were so inextricably bound, had learned Republicanism from his mentor, Chancellor George Wythe of Virginia. Indeed, one of the reasons Clay decided to cross the mountains to Kentucky in 1797 was to escape the "Mock Republicanism" of Washington and to find a place "endowing naturally its owners with ease & affluence as well as preserving them from the infection of prodigality & the poison of Aristocracy," a place that "gave promise of freedom from a corrupt and enslaving past." In Kentucky, Prince Hal, with his Jeffersonian principles, quickly became the political hero of the "liberty-bellowing, Indian-killing" frontiersmen.

But Clay's alliance by marriage with the ruling families of Kentucky had also given him opportunities for investments and handsome fees, and for association with Virginia gentlemen who were anything but "mobocrats." These relationships were to attenuate Clay's Jeffersonian leanings more and more as time went on, until his American System was to be virtually a western-oriented version of Federalism. It was the irony of Clay's career and one that was to cost him his lifelong dream, the Presidency, that he was never able to recognize the essential conflict between wealth and Republicanism. The money that permitted him to live so graciously was to become a fateful issue to Clay, and his growing conservatism in this regard was to have a significant effect also upon Crittenden's career. . . .

During the extreme vacillations of the economy of the nation after 1819, Henry Clay should have kept more closely in touch with the money and banking issue in Kentucky. Foreshadowing its appearance as a national issue, it tore Kentucky apart during the 1820s and precipitated a constitutional crisis centered on the court of appeals. Had Clay's duties and the advice of his friends permitted him to take more interest in this struggle, he might have been better prepared for the rise, under Jackson, of the equalitarian forces, whose power he so consistently underestimated. In his early spectacular western Republicanism, which had made him the Cock of Kentucky to his eastern associates, Clay had militantly followed the course of Jeffersonian democracy; but as the mantle of leadership fell more snugly about his shoulders, he seemed to expect that the westerners would be guided by his judgment as to what was for their welfare. With his own personal associations and his own experiences assuring him of the long-range wisdom of his course, Clay could not see that his American System, with its tariffs, internal improvements, strong military establishments, and central banking, was very like the original Federalism against which he had tilted so vehemently. That his followers should realize this better than he, and that westerners should decide to follow leadership more consistent with the original principles of Republicanism, should have surprised Clay only if he were beguiled into believing the democratic farmer was following him on the road to economic conservatism. Clay would have profited by sharing the experiences of his friend Crittenden in Kentucky's struggle over "relief."

The end of the Napoleonic wars in 1815 brought prosperity to America. Then, as European industry and agriculture recovered sufficiently to reduce their needs for the products of the American West, and as American businessmen saw foreign markets disappearing, cautious lenders resumed the demand for payment in specie that struck at the heart of the war-induced inflation. Lost markets combined with tightened currency to produce the usual effect—sudden and devastating depression. As early as 1818, financial troubles began to appear in the East. The fall was in proportion to the dizzy heights the inflationary spiral had attained. Bankruptcies came on an enormous scale to business houses both in Europe and in America. Sales of western lands dwindled, and land prices plummeted, as did prices for crops, manufactured goods, and slaves. A house and lot on Limestone Street in Lexington, which had been bought for $15,000 a few years before, sold under the hammer for $1,300. Slaves whose hire brought in a hundred dollars the year before sold for only three or four hundred dollars. Corn was selling at ten cents a bushel, and wheat for twenty cents. The depression had come.

Bankers, who had tried vainly to stem the expansion, were already under attack for their conservative policies. Until 1818 there had been only two banks operating in Kentucky: the Bank of the United States, with branches at Louisville and Lexington, and the Bank of Kentucky, about a fifth of whose stock was owned by the state and a majority of whose directors were chosen by the legislature. Although the great mass of people had been suspicious of banknotes since their experience with Continental currency a few decades before, they were now resentful because not enough currency was available. The huge expansion of business immediately after the war led to such pressure by small businessmen for an expanded currency that the legislature in 1818 chartered forty-six banks, soon to be known as the Forty Thieves. Total capitalization of these banks was nearly $9,000,000, almost none of it in specie. Their practice was to issue a flood of notes, lend these out to purchasers of land or for other speculative schemes, and, on the strength of mortgages to secure these loans, issue more banknotes to lend to an ever-growing army of speculators.

But the branches of the Bank of the United States would not accept the notes of these flimsy creatures, and consequently their notes circulated at a huge discount. There was widespread resentment of the Bank of the United States during the boom years for this restrictive policy. A goodly portion of the population of Kentucky was interested in speculation, and a resolution was offered in the legislature in 1819 calling for a tax of $60,000 annually on each branch of the national bank. Another resolution called on the bank to close its Kentucky branches.

When the bubble burst at the end of the boom, public opinion reversed itself. Now the obliging Forty Thieves, who had resisted the attempts of the Bank of the United States to curtail their unsound notes, were themselves the object of the ire of the people and the legislature. The legislature annulled the charters of the Forty Thieves, but the damage had already been done. Debts caused by the collapse of speculative enterprises were staggering. Gross debts due all banks amounted to an estimated $10,000,000, much of it owed by small farmers and mechanics. Now the debtors and many others, feeling the pinch of depression, called public meetings to urge a special legislative session to pass relief measures. Jeffersonian hostility toward strong government, prominent in prosperity, was not so strong in times of depression and want.

Public clamor was difficult for a democratically chosen body to resist. When the legislature met, it created a second state bank, the Bank of the Commonwealth, with a capital stock of $2,000,000, and with authority to issue $3,000,000 in notes not redeemable in specie, for the bank had no specie. Instead, $2,000,000 of its notes were secured only by state stock in the Bank of Kentucky, and by the promise to redeem from receipts of future taxation and from sale of state-owned lands west of the Tennessee River. Loans were limited to $1,000, except that directors might borrow twice that amount, and could be obtained simply by personal endorsement if the borrower had no real estate to mortgage. All borrowers must swear to use the loan either to pay debts or to purchase domestic products. The bank's president and board of directors were chosen annually by the legislature, and they were given great discretion both in making loans and in determining when to call payments.

Crittenden was elected president of the bank, and Francis Preston Blair treasurer. As soon as notes could be prepared, they were distributed to branches to be put in circulation. The legislature took stock, money, and business away from its stable financial institution, the Bank of Kentucky, and hoping to buoy the new institution by the superior credit of the old, sought to have the Bank of Kentucky accept the Commonwealth banknotes at par. Crittenden attempted to work out such an arrangement with his friend John Harvie, president of the Bank of Kentucky. But Harvie, fearing the credit of his own institution would be endangered, agreed only to token acceptance.

From the very beginning, Commonwealth banknotes depreciated, first to seventy cents on the dollar, then to sixty, soon to forty, and even lower outside the state. Moreover, the transfer of state business to the new bank threatened the old; and its notes declined also, although not so rapidly as those of the new bank. Even so, Crittenden and his directors tried various schemes to remedy this decline. First they reduced the number and size of loans and increased interest rates to as high as 2 percent per month. When this did not succeed, they began in 1823, with the legislature's permission, to refuse new loans and to retire the notes as they came back into the bank. At the beginning of 1824 three-quarters of a million dollars were destroyed in public bonfires in the streets of Frankfort, and at the end of that year another half million. By that time the bank had stopped making any new loans, confining its activities to collections of loans already made. These practices soon brought the value of the notes remaining in circulation on a par with those of the Bank of Kentucky.

Although the experiment of the Bank of the Commonwealth was a departure from sound economic policies of the time, it was not a complete failure. That the bank had issued notes without a cent of specie, had made possible the payments of debts and taxes when the notes were heavily discounted, and yet had wound up with its notes at par seemed to many to defy the laws of economics. "A miracle," sneered one of its critics, "whereby something was made out of nothing." Those who felt that this new banking experiment would halt speculation or improve economic conditions were soon disappointed, however.

Another relief measure of 1820 involving the Bank of the Commonwealth was a stay law, which provided that if a creditor should agree to accept notes either of the Bank of the Commonwealth or of the Bank of Kentucky, he might execute judgment on his claim after three months. If he refused, however, the debtor might replevy execution for two years. As the new bank's paper sank to a fraction of its value, pulling that of the old along with it, the creditor faced a dilemma: whether to accept part payment in these discounted notes in satisfaction for all the debt or to wait two years, hoping to collect all at the end of that time but facing the risk of new delays or even total loss then. Creditors became highly incensed at this seeming injustice, and raised cries of indignation. They complained that it was folly for the legislature to attempt to "legislate the people out of debt." Debtors, meanwhile, taking advantage of the law and of public sentiment, pressed harsh terms of settlement, and the unhappiness of creditors grew. Some of them refused to make loans, thus contributing further to business stagnation.

Soon the people of the state organized into rival factions, a division paralleling national party alignments. One faction wanted to repeal the obnoxious stay law, the other to sustain it. The antirelief party, opposed to the law, was composed generally of well-to-do farmers, lawyers, and merchants, although its following included some humbler folk. Conversely, the relief party was based on the debtors, most of whom were small farmers and mechanics. Kentucky's ablest political leaders were divided. Some leaders of the relief party were eminent members of the bar: John Rowan and George M. Bibb, former justices of the court of appeals; William T. Barry and Governor John Adair, Crittenden's old comrades on Shelby's staff; and Solomon P. Sharp. Antirelief leaders were of equal eminence: Robert Wickliffe, Ben Hardin, George Robertson, and Thomas Flournoy.

Although the worst of bad times was over by the spring of 1822, the issue produced a crisis in May of that year, when Judge James Clark decided in a case in the Bourbon circuit court that the stay law was unconstitutional and void because it conflicted with state and national constitutional provisions against laws nullifying contractural obligations. Excitement was so great that Governor John Adair called the legislature into special session, and that body cited Clark to appear before it, a step preliminary to impeachment. Clark did not appear but firmly defended his action in a written response. Meanwhile, an appeal from Clark's decision was pending before the court of appeals. In October, 1823, this court, composed of John Boyle, William Owsley, and Benjamin Mills, sustained the Clark opinion, and the rage of the relief party knew no bounds. Public passion was now diverted from Clark to the court, which had dared to overrule and nullify what the people saw as their august will.

A few weeks after the court of appeals handed down its decision, the legislature met and adopted resolutions denouncing the tyranny of the judges. A bill to impeach them secured a majority, although not the two-thirds vote required by the constitution. But the relief party was not through. Its leaders determined to make removing the judges the issue in the election of the succeeding legislature, and during the next six months, all other questions were forgotten while the two parties agitated the state. Mass meetings were held in all sections, and rival candidates harangued the people. In August the relief party triumphed. Not only did it win a majority in each house, but it also chose by an overwhelming majority a governor, Joseph Desha, who favored removal of the judges.

When the newly elected legislature met in December, the three judges were summoned to appear before it and show cause why they should not be removed. Their calm, well-reasoned answers were countered by Rowan, Bibb, and Barry, the high command of the relief party. But when the removal bill was presented, it still could not muster the two-thirds majority required by the constitution. It received only sixty-nine affirmative to thirty-nine negative votes in the house, and its majority was one less than two-thirds in the senate.

Cheated once more of what they regarded as the just rewards of their victory, the relief advocates resorted to the specious device of reorganizing the court. Late at night on Christmas Eve, with Governor Desha on the floor marshaling the relief forces, the house passed a senate bill reorganizing the court of appeals. (The margin was less than two-thirds in both houses, but since this was a simple legislative act, it did not require the same constitutional majority as the more honest impeachment bill.) By this act the old court of appeals was abolished, the three judges with it, and a new court of four judges was created. The new appointees were all relief men: William T. Barry, chief justice, and John Trimble, B. W. Patton, and R. H. Davidge, associates.

The battle was won but the war was not ended. The old court disregarded the reorganization act, claiming it was irregular and unconstitutional. It merely adjourned, planning to meet again in late January. But the new court lost little time in getting down to business. It chose Francis Preston Blair as its clerk; and when Achilles Sneed, clerk of the old court, refused to surrender his records on demand, Blair took them by force. When the old court returned, it resumed jurisdiction of such cases as were brought before it, so that the state was now plagued with the judicial anarchy of two competing courts of last resort. Some lawyers practiced before one, some before the other, and some before both; but the sympathies of at least nine-tenths of them were with the old judges. Meanwhile, the antirelief party in the legislature presented a masterful protest prepared by George Robertson. It was unceremoniously rejected, however, and the lawmakers adjourned in mid-January in great bitterness.

Up to this time Crittenden had been more a bystander than a participant in the struggle. He practiced before the new court in the spring and summer of 1825, and he had even served on a committee appointed by the new judges to draw up rules for the conduct of the court's business. When he failed to appear before the short session held by the old court that spring, his absence was noted, and it was thought that he had joined the relief party. Crittenden, however, hesitated to enter the fray. He had warm and powerful friends in both camps. He had political ambitions, too, and he doubtless would have welcomed an opportunity to emulate his friend Clay, who though privately in sympathy with the antirelief party refused to commit himself publicly and continued to correspond with members of both factions. Clay was in Washington much of the time, but Crittenden was in Frankfort, the vortex of the controversy, and thus could not long remain on the sidelines. In April, when it was publicly stated that Crittenden's sympathies were with the new court, he published a letter placing himself unequivocally on the side of the old court. "I retain," he said, "a firm and decided conviction that the late act of the Legislature to abolish the Court of Appeals and to reorganize it, merely to effect a change of Judges, is unconstitutional."

Although he had feared that taking a stand would affect his political future, Crittenden was in the long run to benefit from his experience with this struggle. Of necessity he became intimately acquainted here with the deep-seated ramifications of economic class conflict, a harbinger of coming national issues. Here, too, he could devise the sort of strategy to deal with these ramifications that would help later in the national political scene. It is not surprising that Crittenden would finally take a stand for a conservative monetary policy. As president of the dubious Bank of the Commonwealth, he had become acquainted with the dangers of unstable and ill-considered currency policies. His close friends, like Clay's, were the Virginia gentlemen ruling Kentucky, naturally a conservative group, even though a number of them were to take the popular relief side. Further, as the issue came to involve a respect for the law and for the integrity of the courts, Crittenden's natural affection for order and stability would lead him to decide in their favor. Great, indeed, might have been Clay's reward had he been forced to think through the close relationship between economics and politics and to estimate consequences before he made his later decisions on national policy.

Crittenden's avowal was stout support for the antirelief party, who now took on the name Old Court; their adversaries became popularly known as the New Court party. Franklin County was dominated by members of the New Court party, and in order to overcome their preponderance, Crittenden was urged to become a candidate for the legislature. At thirty-eight he was a distinguished public man. He was very popular in Frankfort as lawyer, statesman, and orator, and he was thought to be the only man who had a chance of carrying the Old Court party to victory there. Never a bitter partisan, he had done little thus far to antagonize the opposition. "Crittenden is a man of fine genius," wrote Joseph R. Underwood, and even New Court Clerk Blair, the strongest of partisans, admitted that Crittenden was "a man whose public & private worth has endeared him to all men of all sides in Kentucky."

Franklin County was entitled to two representatives in the house. When Crittenden announced for one of the seats, the New Court party looked about to find candidates who could counter his "great abilities." They found them in Solomon P. Sharp, veteran legislator, congressman for two terms during Madison's administration, and one of the ablest lawyers of the state, and in Lewis Sanders. Thus, three candidates were contending for the two seats.

The New Court men held that although the constitution provided for a court of appeals, its makeup was left to the legislature. Thus, it was a creature of the legislature and, as such, could be abolished by it. To this, Crittenden and his party replied that the judges should hold office during good behavior and could only be removed by impeachment of a two-thirds majority in each house of the legislature. The New Court men countered that the constitution also provided that judges' tenure was limited, not only by good behavior, but by "the continuance of their respective courts." Frequently in the past, they said, circuit courts had been abolished and judges had lost their places, and no one had ever charged that this was a violation of the fundamental law. Conceding this, Crittenden and his associates still contended that legislative power to abolish circuit courts did not extend to the court of appeals.

As the campaign progressed, the New Court party pointed to the repeal of the Federal Judiciary Act of 1801, whereby Jefferson had left many of John Adams' "midnight judges" without a court to preside over. They appealed to Jefferson himself, in retirement at Monticello, to speak out in their support. Although he refused, he was thought to be in sympathy with the New Court principles.

The contest grew bitter as election day neared, for the court issue was symbolic of a deeper conflict. Crittenden was noted for his good temper and equanimity, and at the outset he had presented himself more as a "mediator between contending parties" than as a partisan himself. He had early proposed that a compromise be agreed on whereby all members of both courts would resign and a third court be made up of judges not identified with either party. This was strange doctrine for one who considered the reorganization bill a violation of the constitution, and leaders of the Old Court party would have none of it. In a speech on July 4, however, he repudiated this suggestion; thereafter, according to an adversary, his speeches "assumed by degree a different character." They no longer contained the harmonious sentiments that had so endeared him to all, but breathed "a spirit of denunciation more and more implacable." Crittenden's views were hardening under the heat of battle.

The election in Kentucky was made even more bitter because hard times had increased the litigation over land titles, and many pioneer Kentuckians and naive settlers lost their farms to speculators. Victims of land suits had long resented the courts, and now people saw them as protectors of speculators and of banks, intent on oppressing the poor. The violent feeling aroused here was later to have its counterpart in the whole of the United States, much to the chagrin of Henry Clay.

The 1825 election throughout the state was an astonishing victory for the Old Court party. Sharp and Crittenden were returned to Franklin's two seats, Sharp polling sixty-nine more votes than Crittenden. Fraud was charged on both sides, and with good reason, for in Franklin County alone there were two hundred more votes cast than there were qualified voters.

Although he occasionally resorted to invective in the heat of the contest, Crittenden thought of himself as a mediator. The relief party still regarded him as a restraining influence on the antirelief majority in the legislature, whereas the latter expected him to take the lead in undoing the radical relief legislation of recent years. His problem was not a simple one. The Old Court faction would have a large majority in the lower house, but the senate, where only a fourth of the members were elected annually, was about evenly divided. What if the senate should reject, or the governor veto, a bill to repeal the reorganizing act? Crittenden sought advice from Clay. Would it be wise, he asked, to declare by house resolution that Boyle, Owsley, and Mills were the rightful judges, have them resume their offices, and forcefully repossess themselves of the records taken from them by Blair? Or would it be better to refrain from extreme measures, wait another year, then appeal to the voters at the following election? Clay, as might be expected of the Great Pacificator, urged conciliation. But before any measures could be taken to harmoniously restore a constitutional judiciary, a new sensation was to rekindle tempers that might have subsided.

In the early hours of the very morning the legislature was to convene, Crittenden's colleague from Franklin County, Solomon P. Sharp, who lived only a stone's throw from Crittenden, was awakened from sleep and, in the presence of his wife, savagely stabbed to death by an assassin. The cry went up that the Old Court party had instigated the murder. Violence, which had threatened more than once during the campaign, now seemed ready to blaze all over the state. Into this crisis Crittenden stepped.

When the house assembled a few hours later, Crittenden presented resolutions deploring the assassination and offering a reward of $3,000 for the capture of the murderer. Both were unanimously adopted. But in the shock of the tragedy, coming so close on the heels of the bitter political struggle, wild rumors began to circulate. Sharp was perhaps the ablest member of the New Court party who had been returned to the legislature, and it was soon whispered that his killing was inspired by his political enemies. The finger of suspicion pointed to Jeroboam Beauchamp as the assassin. He had been seen in Frankfort the night before the murder and had asked directions to Sharp's house.

Beauchamp was apprehended and brought back to Frankfort, whence he had fled. He sought Crittenden's aid as counsel. It was not often that Crittenden refused to aid a man in difficulty with the law, but this time he declined. For him to have done otherwise would, under the circumstances, have given strong support to the suspicion that the crime had a political motive.

The sensational trial and resulting revelations showed that the killing had nothing to do with politics. Beauchamp's wife admitted that prior to her marriage to Beauchamp she had borne Sharp's child. Sharp had refused to marry her, she said, and when she made bastardy charges against him, he contended that the child could not be his, for it was black. This had so humiliated and embittered her that she had married Beauchamp only upon his promise to kill Sharp. After making these admissions, she took her life in her husband's cell on the day set for his execution. Because of the bitter political struggle, however, the picture was not so clear-cut. It was charged by Old Court partisans that Governor Desha visited Beauchamp daily in his cell and promised him a pardon if he would implicate leaders of the Old Court party in a conspiracy to take Sharp's life. One of the principal witnesses against Beauchamp was Patrick Darby, editor and Old Court partisan. Beauchamp charged that Darby had testified falsely and had also bribed others to do so. As he was being led to the gallows, he repudiated this and exonerated Darby, but many either did not know of or did not credit this confession.

Meanwhile, the court struggle went on. Leaders of the New Court party, dejected after the August election, had at first seemed inclined to surrender. But when they learned of the balance of parties in the senate, they reconsidered, hoping to obtain better terms. The governor recommended in his message that judges of both courts resign, promising that if they would, he would appoint a new court made up equally of both parties. But the Old Court leaders, unwilling to accept half a loaf, would not agree. They pushed through a bill in the house repealing the reorganization act, but the bill was killed in the senate by the vote of the lieutenant governor.

In the meantime, the Old Court, thinking the issue had been decided by the August election, reassembled in November and prepared to resume business. They sent an order to Blair to deliver up the records in his custody, but Blair refused. With a belligerency that belied his emaciated appearance, he enlisted assistance, procured muskets, kept around-the-clock vigil in his office, and defied the order of the court. He would surrender the records, he said, only to a court reorganized according to the governor's plan. For a time this plan seemed to hold promise. A bill establishing a court made up equally of both parties was proposed. But a fight on the floor of the house between Ben Hardin and Joseph Haskins, a New Court partisan from Mercer County, so inflamed tempers that no such bill could carry.

In this impasse a committee of six from both houses, with Crittenden as chairman, was chosen to work out an adjustment. But even this group could not reach agreement, and on December 21 Crittenden so reported to the house. His own position was now considerably more definite, perhaps as a result of Blair's belligerence. He peremptorily rejected Governor Desha's proposal, or any other that did not admit the unconstitutionality of the act abolishing the Old Court. "If we are right in supposing that the Legislature has no power to abolish the Court," he said, "... we cannot be wrong in rejecting such a compromise, if, indeed, a *compromise* it can be called."

When the legislature adjourned, the courts were in a condition approaching anarchy. Crittenden blamed the failure to resolve the difficulty on the "obstinacy & perverseness" of the governor and a few senators, and he looked forward to the next election, when the people would have an opportunity to remove some of the recalcitrant senators.

But Crittenden was not to have a voice in the final settlement. He campaigned vigorously for reelection, but the New Court majority in Franklin was large, and Crittenden, by his ultimate refusal to support the compromise that he had earlier advocated, lost what support he formerly had secured from New Court advocates. In the

August election he ran third behind Lewis Sanders and David White, who defeated him by 112 and 89 votes respectively.

In the state generally, however, the story was different. The Old Court party won a clear majority, and when the legislature convened, it repealed the act abolishing the old court and restored the old judges to full authority. The governor vetoed the act, but the legislature passed it over his veto. The court struggle thus ended, with the relief advocates defeated and discredited. But the bitterness and factionalism which it aroused were to survive and to be reflected for decades to come in political division on other issues.

Defeat, the first he had ever suffered at the hands of his constituents, was a blow to Crittenden, as it always is to the man of ambition, no matter how experienced and broad-minded. From his loss at the polls, however, came hard-won lessons about American politics. Crittenden was beginning now to understand the power and intransigence of the backwoods farmer, who would not abandon allegiance to Jeffersonian democracy, however clear and overwhelming another cause appeared to his political leaders. Crittenden was also learning the penalty for allowing oneself to become definitely identified over a long period with a conservative faction, a lesson the Federalists had learned long ago in Kentucky. Crittenden knew also, as does every politicain, that to be effective in politics, he must get himself or his candidate elected. He now was beginning to see that the conservatives were a minority in America and could achieve power only by coalition with some other group. Moreover, Crittenden was beginning to appreciate the necessity of careful strategy and vigorous and skillful conduct of political campaigns, a lesson to be pointed up in 1840. He had also discovered something of the chicanery that was coming increasingly to be practiced at the polls in American elections; the vote in his own county was evidence of this. All of these insights, gained by Crittenden from bitter experience, would have profited Clay greatly.

(from John J. Crittenden: The Struggle for the Union, *pp. 46-47, 49-63)*

NOSTALGIA FOR A MYTH

The war was to have an even more subtly sinister effect on the South than the deterioration of race relations. The flamboyant corruption and vulgarity of the black and tan governments were to play into the hands of provincial minded Southerners by offering convincing proof that their own way of life and political philosophy were infinitely superior to Yankee practices. The replacing of the old, and at least outwardly genteel, order by the new, left in the survivors a nostalgia for a society that never was, but which grew in their imaginations as the ante-bellum period receded into the past. One Southern scholar calls this impact of Reconstruction on the Southern mind more damaging in the long run than all the more tangible effects of excessive taxation and misgovernment. It made of the Confederacy, he said, a ghost which haunted the imagination of the South.

It was this nostalgia for a myth that was to breed hostility and resistance to change and progress. Change in either values or mores would constitute disloyalty to the sacred dead. Progress of any kind would mean change, and thus it must be eschewed. The South must remain agrarian. It must go on growing cotton. The Negro must be kept servile. Fundamentalism in religion must be clung to. Writing in the 1870s Sidney Lanier despaired of the future of his native Southland. The people, he thought, had failed to perceive the deeper movements under-running the times. "They lie wholly off," he wrote, "out of the stream of thought, and whirl their poor dead leaves of recollection round and round in a piteous eddy that has all the wear and tear of motion without any of the rewards of progress."

(from "The Defeated," a paper read before the Mississippi Valley Historical Association, Louisville, April 29, 1960)

DEMAGOGUERY AND REFORM

... Many of the "demagogues" were race-baiters; others lacked a program, or the ability to put one through once they gained office. Some, with good intentions, were hopelessly confused as to what needed to be done. Some were charlatans and scoundrels who once they gained office sold out to the interests who opposed them. But the best of them—Long, Vardaman, and even Bilbo—worked for the best interests of the people whom they represented and who trusted them. Southern political history, confusing at best, is hopelessly confounded by too free usage of the term demagogue. It would be better to forget the word altogether and to classify politicians, if indeed they must be classified, as reformers or non-reformers, as progressives or conservatives. For although these terms are sweeping and subjective too, they do avoid evaluation of motives, a thing not often possible, and permit judgments on the politicians' accomplishments rather than on their supposed beliefs.

(from The South since Appomattox, *p. 129)*

DEMAGOGUERY EVALUATED

It must not be forgotten that there was much more to Vardaman's program than its racial feature. For decades there had been a crying need for social reform, but the old-style politician went blindly on his way, paying lip service to the majesty of the people but doing nothing to alleviate their lot. There was convincing evidence that the state was controlled by political "rings" rotten to the core. Huge treasury deficits were discovered in 1890 and again in 1901. Moreover, the "rings" seemed to be in an alliance with the new business interests, which the farmers regarded as the source of all their troubles. In 1882 new railroads and manufactures had been exempted from taxes for a term of ten years. This had been, the farmers thought, but an opening wedge for newer and greater concessions later. It had become customary for politicians to rant against corporations, but little action had been taken to allay their monopolistic grip. Finally, in 1900 at his inaugural, Longino was honest, bold, or stupid enough to express an open friendship for them. He hoped, he said, that "no more sentimental or prejudicial opposition to railroads or other corporate enterprises will find favor with the legislature. Two years later he was pleased to report that "there exists ... a becoming liberality of sentiment by the masses toward the corporate and other investments of money in our midst."

Vardaman and other "demagogues" did not think so. It was against these interests, as well as against the Negro, that they directed their campaigns. Since they were fighting these interests, the chief publicity agency, the press, was opposed to them. Suffering under this handicap they had to resort to vivid and dramatic campaign tactics in order to publicize themselves. Their appeal was directed to poor as against rich, to farmer as against townsman, to the "common man" as against the aristocrat. Poverty, as A. B. Moore observes, seems to make the masses "susceptible to demagogic appeals." Frequently, he says, "people have turned ... for relief to the so-called demagogues." But it is too easy for those who control agencies of publicity to condemn their opponents as "demagogues." "Whether one is to be classed as a demagogue or a statesman seems to depend quite often upon the respectability of his followers and upon the agencies of propaganda which support or oppose him." Thus, Burkitt was denounced as a "demagogue" when he allegedly advocated Negro voting, and Vardaman was similarly denounced when he advocated greater safeguards against Negro voting. It is a remarkable coincidence that, despite their radical differences on the Negro question, Vardaman inherited Burkitt's following. This would tend to belie the charge that Vardaman's success was due to his Negro baiting alone.

"A demagogue," says Gerald W. Johnson, "is objectionable for a vast number of reasons, but he has at least the virtue of being alive; and when the choice lies between a demagogue and a political corpse," the voters must choose the former. The old "respectable" Democratic leaders recognized no social responsibility other than the negative one of preventing "negro domination." That provided, they considered their duty done. Generally their rule was honest but selfish. Its gentility was enjoyed at the cost of the neglect of the social welfare of the masses of the population. It was not until the "demagogues" Vardaman and Bilbo awakened the social consciousness of the people that any constructive social legislation was enacted in Mississippi. Vardaman started the ball rolling with his crusade against unspeakable conditions existing in the penitentiary and other state institutions. Bilbo carried it further with his commission to eliminate adult illiteracy, a law to curb the textbook trust, the furnishing of transportation for children in the rural consolidated schools, and the passage of a compulsory school-attendance law. Under his administration, too, laws were passed curbing the activities of corporations and the sale of bogus stocks, regulating public utilities, and breaking the insurance trust. He sponsored the building of hospitals and institutions for the subnormal, game and fish laws, temperance, laws to eradicate ticks and tuberculosis from cattle, estate and inheritance taxes, a tax-equalization commission, antilobbying laws, and the elimination of public hangings.

These accomplishments may not establish Vardaman and Bilbo as great statesmen, but they should tend to offset the charge of "demagoguery" which has been so generally hurled at them by the "respectable" press. If these reforms were effected by corrupt means, as was so generally charged of Bilbo, that is merely the price that has to be paid when reforms are neglected until a man of Bilbo's type comes to power. The astonishing thing, as Gerald Johnson points out, was the conservatism of the programs of these "wild men" and the bitterness and hatred which the "wild men" provoked in the "respectable" people. Instead of turning the affairs of state into chaos, as was freely predicted, all they advocated and gained was what was generally regarded in other sections "as the merest routine of good government. Roads, schools, public health service, the imposition of taxes on those best able to pay." The success of both Vardaman and Bilbo is proof of the inadequacy of the kind of government in Mississippi before them. "Call these men demagogues if you will," says Ray Stannard Baker speaking of southern "demagogues" in general, ". . . they yet represent a genuine movement for a more democratic government in the South."

As for the Negro, whose presence in such large numbers in Mississippi has given such a distinctive influence to its politics, his lot did not change throughout the period. No one thought of him save to hold him down. No one sought to improve him. Whether race baiters like Vardaman were in power, or whether "respectable" politicians governed, he fared the same—no better, no worse. He was and is the neglected man in Mississippi, though not the forgotten man.

(from Revolt of the Rednecks, *pp. 312-14)*

THE GREAT CRUSADE AND AFTER

The coming of the Second World War ended for a time the liberal-conservative cleavages in the South over the New Deal. No other section gave the President more united support in his efforts to aid Britain in the 1940-41 period of neutrality. The America First Committee, an organization whose aim was to keep the United States out of war, scored no gains in the South. Draft extension and the revised neutrality act would have been defeated without the all-but-unanimous support of southern Representatives and Senators. The internationalist sentiment of the South during the period was a reflection of the peculiar social and economic conditions prevailing there. The ruin of cotton export trade was balanced by the $10 billion which the federal government poured into the section for defense plants, although the presence of these same plants would promote an isolationist sentiment in the postwar years. In October 1941, however, 88 percent of southerners polled thought it was more important that Germany be defeated than that the United States stay out of the European war. This in contrast to the approximately 63 percent of Americans in other regions who favored intervention.

But the New Deal and the Great Depression combined with World War II wrought profound changes in southern society. The nation rediscovered how backward the region was and undertook to remake it, a move that provoked resentment among southerners. Such phrases as "economic problem number one" and "reactionary southerners" caused bitterness in the South against northerners, as also did controversies over segregation in the armed forces. Then, too, anti-racial propaganda during the war with Hitler made white supremacists uneasy. As Jasper B. Shannon has pointed out, the Negro with a job and with a wartime FEPC to protect it, was unwilling to accept his former position in southern society. Besides, millions of southern whites and Negroes during the war had served in other sections of the country and even in foreign lands, where southern traditions were not a way of life. This experience doubtless changed the attitude of many of them toward southern racial mores.

Until Roosevelt's capture of the northern Negro vote in 1933, the South had felt secure on the race issue. But when the northern Negro shifted to the Democratic party both national parties sought his vote, offering platform inducements that would not be tolerated in the South. By the mid-1930's it was clear that the votes of northern and eastern states were vital to Democratic success nationally, while southern votes no longer were. Realization of this in the post-World War II era eroded southern loyalty to the party and renewed the former controversy between conservatives and liberals in the South. . . .

In 1948, President Harry Truman made civil liberties the central point of his program, and southern conservatives went into open revolt against him. In contrast to 1928 when the hard core of Democratic loyalty was in the rural, black-country regions, the center of the opposition to Truman was in the black belt. The revolt had its beginning in 1944 when the Mississippi Democratic convention placed uninstructed electors on the party ballot. The hope then had been that other states would follow the example and that a large bloc of uninstructed southern electors might in a close election seize the balance of power. The Mississippi plot had been defeated, however, when the legislature, under Bilbo's influence, nominated another slate of electors pledged to Roosevelt. These had soundly defeated the anti-Roosevelt group. It would have been madness for Mississippians to have bolted after this, for Roosevelt was sure to win without them. Only Texas conservatives adopted the Mississippi plan, and there also the regulars won.

By 1948, Roosevelt was dead, and the Congressional elections of 1946 had given encouragement to Republicans and southern conservatives alike. . . . On July 17 the adjourned Jackson Convention reconvened at Birmingham as planned and organized the States Rights, or Dixiecrat party. Senator J. Strom Thurmond of South Carolina was nominated for President and [Fielding] Wright for Vice President. Their expectations rested on the hope that northern Democrats would favor a southern Democrat over a Republican, and that Republicans would favor a southern over a northern Democrat. The Dixiecrats did not expect to win the election. Their strategy was to prevent either Truman or Thomas E. Dewey, the Republican candidate, from getting a majority of the Electoral vote and thus throw the election into the House of Representatives. The prospect was enhanced by Henry Wallace's candidacy on the Progressive ticket.

In the campaign that followed, the liberal-conservative battle in the South was fought to a showdown; the liberal wing supporting Truman, the conservative Thurmond. . . .

The election proved a shock to southern Dixiecrats. Their plan would have succeeded if Texas, Arkansas, Georgia, and Florida had been carried. But Truman's hard campaigning, Dewey's overconfidence, and Wallace's complete ineffectiveness proved their undoing. Also, too many southern Democratic politicians who privately wished the movement well feared retaliation if they joined the Dixiecrats, and the Democrats won. Another factor in Dixiecrat failure was fear of loss of Congressional seniority by southern Congressmen if they should bolt.

The Dixiecrat split brought the influence of southerners in the national Democratic party to ebb tide. Henceforth, the section would have even a smaller voice in national affairs. Too late, conservative southerners realized their mistake in 1936 in permitting elimination of the two-thirds rule in nominating conventions. Thereafter, the section could neither rule nor ruin. Furthermore, it was apparent that a cleavage had come now between the deep South and the upper South. Truman carried the upper South and the election in 1948 while losing four of the deep South states. The South had also moved a great distance from pre-New Deal political patterns. Capture of the cotton textile industry by the South and capture of the northern Negro vote by the Democratic party began the process that was to free southern conservatives from unquestioning loyalty to the national Democratic party. For the textile industry brought to the South inclinations toward a protective tariff not unlike traditional northern Republican tariff concepts. This, together with Roosevelt's and Truman's wooing of the northern Negro vote, weakened the South's historic devotion to the Democratic party. . . .

By 1940, southern industry was already over twice as valuable as its agriculture. Fierce competition between communities for new factories and more jobs was bringing new interests which dimmed if they did not actually drive out old loyalties.

Under these economic pressures, regional cohesion was pulling apart, so that the Negro question was left as the sole unifying force. This was a powerful force, which a two-party system doubtless would help abate, but the end of which could not yet be seen. Nevertheless, the economic revolution was producing a social revolution, which in turn was eroding many old beliefs and customs that had held back the section. Cultural influences, together with news media, especially radio and television, were nationalizing American society, and this was having political implications. Group and class conflicts crossed sectional lines, and these conflicts were forcing political parties to adopt national programs to deal with them. Rural southern Democrats, even Dixiecrats, were often sectional only on race. On other issues they frequently were allied with rural people in other sections, most of whom were Republicans. This alliance of rural politicians rested largely on the mutual antipathy both groups had toward urban people, but such antipathy was greatly exaggerated.

The so-called coalition in Congress between southern Democrats and northern Republicans was largely a myth; for except on issues dealing directly with race or with extension of federal powers which might lead to tampering with race relations, southern Congressmen from urban districts and Senators with large urban populations such as Tennessee, Florida, and Texas voted almost invariably with northern Democrats on party measures. It was the rural southerner and the rural northern Republican who were responsible for creating the illusion of an alliance. On almost everything but racial issues, southern and northern industrialists found they had more in common than either had with his workers, just as northern and southern doctors, farmers, teachers, workers, businessmen also found much common ground. Furthermore, widespread prosperity which accompanied industrialization and urban growth in the South showed signs of breaking down the apathy of the masses toward politics, education, and labor. The ending of the poll tax in some states, together with the outlawing of the white primary everywhere, was contributing mightily toward increased political activity by these masses.

If the South was more conservative than the rest of the country then, it was because it was more rural. But there was more to it than this. Rural areas in all sections were over-represented in state legislatures, but this was more true of the South than of other regions. And democracy in the South consequently was beset with a conservatism begotten not only of an undemocratic rural control of state legislatures but one in which the ruling rural minority had a historical dedication to the county as a unit of government. The undemocratic nature of Georgia's county unit system in electing state officers has already been noted. Equally inequitable was her legislative apportionment. Fulton County (Atlanta) had about a fifth of the population of the state but elected only 1 of 54 state senators and 3 of more than 200 representatives. Similarly, Jefferson County, Alabama (Birmingham), had more than 20 percent of the state's population but elected only 1 of 35 senators and 7 of 106 representatives. The southern half of Alabama, dominated by the black belt, had far less than half the state's population and wealth and paid less taxes proportionately on its property. Yet it had a majority in both houses, a majority chosen by a minority, as has been shown, invariably dominated by its own white minority dedicated to the preservation of the status quo. Sometimes this rural minority was joined by urban conservatives, eager to retain the rural majority in the legislature so that white supremacy would be preserved or union labor subdued. This coalition of conservatives from rural and urban areas stubbornly refused to permit reapportionment, despite state laws requiring that it be done every decade.

(from The South since Appomattox, *pp. 286-87, 292, 294-97)*

ON THE INTERNATIONAL CRISIS

One cannot spend as much time in any institution as I have spent in this one without noting many changes that occur through the different student generations. When I was a student here in the mid-1920s the university was small, and there was an informal, relaxed, friendly atmosphere, that I think is generally characteristic of the place today. There were few students from outside the state and none from outside the country. There were no black, or brown, or yellow students; all were white. But there were differences of another kind between that age and this—less tangible differences but nevertheless of striking importance. Our world at that time, our society was stable and secure. "The war to end wars" had been won; indeed it was still known as The Great War, for there was yet no reason to designate it the First World War. The prosperity of the period gave us little concern for our future economic security. Success for our generation seemed assured.

Since those halcyon days great events have wrought profound changes. First in order of time, the Great Depression of the 1930s, brought many troubles: economic uncertainty, even doubts as to the survival of the social order. Finding a job and fear of future insecurity placed a damper on the spirits of all young people. On the whole, the high school and college generation of the 1930s was a rather sad, depressed, unadventurous generation.

Then came the Second World War. That war, unlike the present one, did not split the nation. It was regarded as "a just war," and young people, as well as their elders, were joined in their support of the united effort. But conditions for college students were quite abnormal. The ratio of about 2½ or 3 men to women on campus was suddenly reversed, and extracurricular and social activity was greatly curtailed. It was a period of dullness that was relieved only by a feeling of suspense and of great uncertainty.

The Second World War was soon followed by another period almost equally dark—"The McCarthy Era." Spurred on by the crusading Senator from Wisconsin, the feeling grew that a worldwide communist conspiracy threatened America with overthrow from within. Government officials with long records of honorable service were harried and persecuted; and a few, whose patriotism seemed until then above question, were actually proved disloyal. Students' and professors' lives were not unmarked by these events. A feeling of apprehension about what they thought and said—with whom they should not associate, what organizations they should join caused many to live in a quite unAmerican manner marked by fear of persecution.

And so we come to the 1960s, a decade which in many respects is similar to that of my own student days in the 1920s. The unparalleled prosperity of the past and present years inspires no fear of economic or professional insecurity. McCarthyism is discredited, freedom of thought and speech firmly re-established. But yet there are certain marked differences between this generation of college students and my own more than 40 years ago.

For one thing, the certainty of the future of the country and of the world order is no longer taken for granted. Today, in our own country, we see an increasingly affluent society cheek-by-jowl with less privileged groups who are thrust aside and who exist in stagnant pools outside the mainstream of the American social order. The refusal of Negroes, who are a large portion of this group, to accept their conditions spurred civil rights and social welfare legislation which have been landmarks of the past 5 years. But the failure of this legislation to materially improve the life of the poor has raised questions as to the value of the programs and have pointed to the need for new appraisals of the problems.

Meanwhile, the quality of city life is deteriorating. As the rural poor from the South and from Appalachia move into the cities the well-to-do move out to the subdivisions. Property values decline, and neither the city nor the state governments can raise the vast sums needed to improve housing and schools in the ghettoes. Only the federal government has the potential to raise the money needed to pay for this vast rehabilitation if our cities and our society are to be preserved from ruin. Meanwhile, federal funds, talents, energies have been directed toward other projects with higher priorities; the fighting of the Cold War, Vietnam, and the space program.

The present disarray in American society and in world society is forcing us into a reappraisal of these priorities. We are asking ourselves, if it is a question of the slums or of Vietnam which shall come first? And if Vietnam has isolated us politically and morally, from the rest of the world can we afford this in the name of "containing China"? We are asking ourselves if it is wise and moral to spend billions on flight to the moon when so much needs improvement here on earth and in our own beloved land? Do we need to reach the moon first so as to improve our international image vis-a-vis Russia?

So far, I have touched only on our own national problems, problems we can resolve—if we have the will—unilaterally, by making up our own minds, fixing our own priorities, and sticking firmly to them. But there is another problem of world dimensions—one we cannot settle by ourselves. This problem is created by the fact that in many places there are too many people and that population is growing at such a rate—particularly in the undeveloped countries— that soon the earth will be unable to support the people on it. Unless we do something about it, within a few decades—within the life expectancy of all of you—there will be so many people on the earth that the condition will become irreversible.

Through revolutionary developments in the health sciences infant mortality has been radically reduced and human life extended. And this is true in all parts of the world but especially of recent years in the undeveloped countries. This has resulted in adding presently 125 people every minute to the world's population. Every month, at the present rate, 5.5 million people, almost enough to populate Kentucky twice again, is added to the world total. Long before the end of this century there will be at least twice as many people in the world as there are today. At the same time this is happening the gap between the rich and the poor countries is widening. In a large part of the world the per capita income is 1/200 of what it is in this country. Soon it will be 1/300. The seriousness of this situation needs no detailing. The only hope of fending off disaster is that in some way the rate of population increase can be reversed and that food production can be greatly increased. It is really a race between the demographers and the agronomists to speed increased food production so as to prevent famine while they prepare to reverse the birth rate; the agronomists urging the demographers for instant decrease in the birth rate so as to give them a lead time to produce more food in the developing nations.

Now, our problem seems as bald as this: If the catastrophe of famine on a worldwide scale is to be avoided in the next few decades several things must be done:

1) The rich countries must produce more food and technical assistance for the poor countries.

2) The poor countries must make a major effort to revolutionize their own productivity. To succeed in this they must move along industrially. For if they are to turn out more food they need more electrical power to produce fertilizers, to pump water, for refrigeration, and for food processing.

3) Both poor and rich countries must reverse the rate of population increase.

What are the obstacles to be overcome if these objectives are to be attained? They are several and they are formidable. In the first place, if population control is to be effected it must have the support of world opinion. Not only is there considerable opposition to this in the Western World, but in large parts of the Orient it seems that there is an overpowering social drive for couples to be grandparents by their mid-thirties.

In the second place, if the undeveloped countries are to be brought to a condition of self-sufficiency and world famine avoided the rich countries must make sacrifices comparable to those made in wartime. It is estimated that this will require 20% of the United States gross national product for the next decade or two. This will be utterly impossible without a radical decrease in military expenditures. The effect would be that our standard of living for a long period would cease to grow and might actually decline. Furthermore the task is so formidable that it will require the joint efforts of the

United States, Western Europe, and Russia working together to accomplish the necessary results.

Success in the endeavor is therefore predicated on the assumption that the United States and Russia will agree to bring the Cold War to an end; for it is inconceivable that either will disarm unilaterally. Both must face the fact squarely that neither will collapse within the foreseeable future. Both nations must cease to wait for the other to change its social and economic order. For to wait that long before cooperative action would permit world population to double, redouble, and double again.

These are some of the problems your generation must grapple with in the world that you are inheriting: they are problems of mounting difficulties and grave dangers. They will not disappear of themselves with time, but will require affirmative action. To do nothing in the hope that they will go away would be suicidal. They require courageous and far-reaching plans. These plans must be rational, and they must be implemented by traditional methods of constitutional and peaceable change. But change is necessary if we are to avoid violence. For the only basis for national and international peace rests in the confidence of the people in the ability of society to reform itself. But change wrought by violence will solve no problems. Violence will only multiply the problems and increase the misery. The Bible warns those who take up the sword that they may perish by the sword. Riots lead to repression; violence to counter-violence; anarchy calls forth the police state.

In its foreign relations the United States, although one of the super-states, cannot permit itself to become morally and politically isolated. Financial and military power can never be a substitute for moral power. The decent people of the world will not follow the leader who betrays their moral principle. And if they are persuaded that we have abandoned our moral principles the nations of the world will not be impressed by our tall buildings or the power of our machines of war.

Faced with causes of this consequence we must stop being trivial. Compared to this other issues are absurd. And young people who are looking for a cause worthy of their talents will find one here. Your generation has been called by someone "Rebels without a cause." And there is never reason nor justice in blaming present shortcomings in world society on the generation that has preceded you. After all, your parents did not create the world, nor did they inherit a perfect one and then twist it into its present disarray. You must take the world as you find it and do the best you can to make it better. Remember that, in a short time from now, you too will have children to whom you will have to answer for the state of the world you will leave to them as an inheritance.

So the trumpet blows, calling you to the battle. Here is a cause worthy of your greatest fervor. It is the biggest cause in history; larger than the Crusades, the Reformation, the Enlightenment. For survival of the race itself, and civilization as we know it, hangs on the outcome. And of one thing you may be sure: the future of the world will be determined by the manner in which your generation addresses itself to this challenge.

(from address at the University of Kentucky, 1968[?])

Index

Aderholt, O. C., 103
Albright, A. D., 56; excerpt from Kirwan's letter to, 90-94
Angelucci, Ralph, 60
Arntson, Neal, 9
Ashland (estate of Henry Clay), 46
Ashland High School, 24
athletic scholarships, 36, 38-39, 103, 108

basketball scandals, 35-40, 67-68 n.26; Kirwan's statement before SEC executive committee concerning, 102-12
Bell House, 46
Boles, S. A. "Daddy," 13
Brown, Bill, 25
Bryant, Paul "Bear," 35, 37, 39, 41
Butts, Wally, 25, 103
Byers, Walter, 55

Carpenter, J. B., 20
"Cassius Clay's *True American*," 29
Centre College, 10, 13, 14-16, 26
Chamberlain, Leo, 40-41, 96
Chandler, A. B. "Happy," 60-61, 64
Charles S. Sydnor award, 29, 52
Civilization of the Old South: Writings of Clement Eaton, 53
Clark, Thomas D.: as chairman of UK history department, 28-30, 65, 70 n.96; characterizes Kirwan, 32, 33, 42, 45; *The South since Appomattox: A Century of Regional Change* (with Kirwan), 44, 52-53; excerpts from, 139-42, 146-49, 149-53, 153-55, 173, 176-80; and the University Press of Kentucky, 50-54; Kirwan speech honoring tenure of, excerpt from, 98-102
Cochran, Lewis, 54-55, 60
Cone, Carl, 45, 62, 102
Confederacy, 51; excerpts from: "King Cotton," 115-16; "How Did the People Keep Body and Soul Together?" 131-34
Covington, Herb, 16
Creech, Glenwood, 60

Dartmouth Amendment, 36, 106-7, 112
Denbo, Bruce F., 50, 54, 63
Denham, Harry, 61-62, 68 n.27
Dickey, Frank, 54, 55, 56, 61, 85
Donovan, Herman Lee, 29, 30, 85; Kirwan's relationship with, 32; and basketball scandals, 35, 37, 40, 109, 111; *Keeping the University Free and Growing,* 42, 43; excerpt from Kirwan's speech at retirement banquet for, 94-98
Duke University, 30, 32
duPont Manual High School, 8-9, 20, 22, 33, 37

Farquhar, E. F. "Red," 12
football: Kirwan plays, 8-9; Kirwan coaches at duPont Manual, 20, 23-24, 25; at UK, 14-17, 19, 26-29. *See also* names of individual coaches and players
Forth, Stuart, 61, 62-63
Funkhouser, William H., 12

Gallalee, John, 102, 104
Gordy, Minos, 15, 16
Great Teacher Award, 43

INDEX 187

"Green Fly," 33
Gregg, Turner, 15

Heber, John, 17
Heil, John H., Sr., 21
Holmes, Sarah Blanding, 32, 34; dormitory named for, 60
Hopkins, James, 32-33, 43, 53

Jenkins, Paul, 24
John J. Crittenden: The Struggle for the Union, 51, 52, 53, 56; excerpts from: "The Whole Union is Our Country," 116-17; "Toward the Abyss," 118-25; "Old Court-New Court," 159-71
Johnny Green of the Orphan Brigade: The Journal of a Confederate Soldier, 51
Johnson, Clyde "Big Train," 28
Johnson, Tom, 20
Jones, T. T., 30

Keeping the University Free and Growing (Herman Lee Donovan), 42, 43
Kentucky Military Institute: excerpt from Kirwan's commencement address at (1969), 82-84
Kentucky, University of. *See* University of Kentucky
Kirwan, Albert Dennis ("Ab"): origin of nickname, 3; childhood of, 3-7; plays football at Male High School, 8-9; describes campus and academic life at UK, 9-13; plays football at UK, 13-18; as UK backfield coach, 19; combines teaching and coaching at Male with law school, 20; marries Betty Heil, 20-21; practices law, 21-22; as head coach at duPont Manual High School, 22-25; first son born to, 24; as head coach at UK, 26-29; second son born to, 26; teaches history during the war, 28; takes masters degree and doctorate, 29-31; as UK dean of men, 32-35; appointed faculty chairman of athletics, 35; crusades against "sanity code," 36; and basketball scandals, 36-41, 102-12; returns to teaching, 42-44; wins Great Teacher Award, 43; social and personal relationships, 45-46; family life, 46-49; as author and editor, 50-53; wins awards for *John J. Crittenden*, 52; involved in formation of University Press of Kentucky, 53-54; as dean of UK graduate school, 53-60; dormitory named for, 60; as Acting President of UK, 60-64; installed as seventh President of UK, 64-65; death of, 66
— *publications*: *The Revolt of the Rednecks* (1951), 31, 50; excerpts from, 144-46, 173-75; *Johnny Green of the Orphan Brigade: The Journal of a Confederate Soldier* (1956), 51; *The Confederacy* (1959), 51; excerpts from, 115-16, 131-34; *John J. Crittenden: The Struggle for the Union* (1962), 51, 52, 53, 56; excerpts from, 116-17, 118-25, 159-71; *The South since Appomattox: A Century of Regional Change* (with Thomas D. Clark, 1967), 44, 52-53; excerpts from, 139-42, 146-49, 149-53, 153-55, 173, 176-80; *The Civilization of the Old South: Writings of Clement Eaton*, 53; articles and papers (1960), excerpts from: "The Defeated," 134-35, 139, 143-44, 172; "The Kentucky Soldier in the Civil War," 127-28; "The Orphan Brigade," 129-30; "Without Due Process," 126-27
—*speeches*: commencement addresses, at Lafayette High School (1960), 81-82; at Kentucky Military Institute (1969), 82-84; at UK [1968 (?) and 1969], 85-90, 180-85; Donovan retirement banquet speech (1956), 94-98; Phi Alpha Theta banquet speech honoring Thomas D. Clark's tenure as chairman of UK history department (1968), 98-102; statement before executive committee of Southeastern Conference, 102-12

— *letters of, excerpts from:* (March 9, 1970) to Wayman Thomason, discussing history, 84-85; (November 18, 1970) to A. D. Albright, discussing UK policies and programs, 90-94
Kirwan, Albert D., Jr. ("Denny") (son), 24, 46-47
Kirwan, Catherine (sister), 7
Kirwan, Delia Link (daughter-in-law), 49
Kirwan, Edward (great uncle), 3
Kirwan, Edward Emmett (half brother), 3
Kirwan, Elizabeth Heil (wife), 10, 42, 60, 65; marriage to Ab and family life, 21, 31, 45-49, 73; at Bowman Hall, as wife of Dean of Men, 32-33; helps with Ab's research and writing, 50-51; at Maxwell Place, as wife of Acting President, 61
Kirwan, Harry (half brother), 3, 9
Kirwan, Joseph (uncle), 3, 4, 5
Kirwan, Joseph Ross (half brother), 3, 9
Kirwan, Margaret (sister), 4, 8, 10
Kirwan, Margaret Sullivan (mother), 4, 5, 7, 66
Kirwan, Martin John (father), 3-7, 47, 66
Kirwan, Martin John, Jr. (brother), 6
Kirwan, Mary (sister), 7
Kirwan, Mary Elizabeth Ross (grandmother), 3
Kirwan, Patricia Harper (daughter-in-law), 49
Kirwan, Patrick Nolan (grandfather), 3
Kirwan, Susan (sister), 4
Kirwan, William English (brother), 4, 5, 6, 12, 47
Kirwan, William English II ("Brit") (son), 26, 45, 46-49

Lafayette High School: excerpt from Kirwan's commencement address at (1960), 81-82
Lexington Drug (store), 11
Louisville, University of, 20, 22

McCubbin, William, 23
McMillan, Bo, 10, 16
McVey, Frances Jewell (Mrs. Frank LeRond), 13
McVey, Frank LeRond, 13, 25, 26, 33, 85
Male High School, 6, 8-9, 13, 20, 21, 23, 82
Maxson, Ralph N. "Maggie," 12-13
Maxwell Place, 15, 45, 61, 62
Melcher, Columbus Rudolph, 18
Middlesboro High School, 24
Milward, Emmett, 62
Murphy, Fred, 16, 19

National Collegiate Athletic Association (NCAA), 35-36, 44, 52, 55; and basketball scandals, 40-41, 106, 107
National Youth Alliance, 89
Nunn, Governor Louie B., 61-62, 71 n.110, 85

Omicron Delta Kappa, 17, 62
Oswald, John, 35, 61, 85; as President of UK, 56-58, 60; characterization of, 70-71 n.98

Papers of Henry Clay, 53
Peterson, Frank, 95
Phi Alpha Theta: excerpt from Kirwan's speech at banquet honoring Thomas D. Clark, 98-102
Phoenix Hotel, 11, 28
Polis's Restaurant, 11
Prohibition, 11, 19

Revolt of the Rednecks, 31, 50; excerpts from: "Franchise and Apportionment," 144-46; "Demagoguery Evaluated," 173-75
Rhodemyer, Jay, 28
Roberts, Red, 10, 16
Rodes, William "Doc," 16, 26
Royster, Wimberly, 54, 60, 64
Rupp, Adolph, 11, 29, 35, 40-41, 107

"sanity code," 35-36, 106
Shively, Bernie, 26, 35
Sigma Nu, 10-11, 14, 15, 17, 45
Singletary, Otis, 34, 49, 64
Southeastern Conference (SEC), 28, 29, 36; and basketball scandals, 38-40, 102-12

South since Appomattox: A Century of Regional Change (with Thomas D. Clark), 44, 52-53; excerpts from: "The Negro," 139-42; "Southern Labor," 146-49; "Segregation and Black Handicaps," 149-53; "Exit Jim Crow," 153-55; "Demagoguery and Reform," 173; "The Great Crusade and After," 176-80
Streit, Judge Saul: and basketball scandals, 35, 38-40, 110
Sullivan, Grandma, 7
Sydnor, Charles S., 30; award, 29, 52

Talbert, Charles, 25
Tanner, Albert, 14-15, 45
Tennessee, University of, 14-17, 19, 26

University of Kentucky: Kirwan describes campus life, 9-13, 97; fraternities, 10-11, 14, 17, 98, 101; Lamp and Cross, 17; Law School, 18; athletics program, 27, 35, 41 (*see also* athletic scholarships; basketball scandals; football, at UK); history department, 28-29, 42, 98-102; student dissension, 34, 62-64, 87-89; integration of, 34, 97; panty raids, 34-35; *The Kernel*, 43-44; University Press of Kentucky, 44, 50-54; committees, 44, 55; graduate school, 54-60; fellowships and grants, 57-58; research, 58, 92-93; Engineering College, 59; Kirwan discusses admissions policy, 90-92. *See also* Kirwan, Albert D.
University of Louisville, 20, 22
University of Tennessee, 14-17, 19, 26

Weaver, Red, 10
Webb, E. B. "Dick," 14
Webb, William S., 12
Wiles, Howard, 8
Winn, Jack, 15

Xavier High School, 6, 24

Young Americans for Freedom, 89

www.ingramcontent.com/pod-product-compliance
Lightning Source LLC
Chambersburg PA
CBHW021809220426
43662CB00006B/242